PENGUIN HANDBOOKS
BOY, GIRL, MAN, WOMAN

B. H. Claësson was born in 1935 and has been a doctor
since 1963 and a child and youth psychiatrist since
1978. He has been on the staffs of various hospitals and
other institutions, including as a member of departments
of psychiatry. He has also given sex education classes
to the young, and has appeared on many radio and
television programmes on sex education.

B. H. CLAËSSON

Boy, Girl, Man, Woman

A Guide to Sex for Young People

Translated by Christine Hauch

*New English edition revised
by Angela Phillips*

Penguin Books

Penguin Books Ltd, Harmondsworth,
Middlesex, England
Penguin Books, 625 Madison Avenue,
New York, New York 10022, U.S.A.
Penguin Books Australia Ltd, Ringwood,
Victoria, Australia
Penguin Books Canada Ltd, 2801 John Street,
Markham, Ontario, Canada L3R 1B4
Penguin Books (N.Z.) Ltd, 182–190 Wairau Road,
Auckland 10, New Zealand

Originally published in Danish as DRENG OG PIGE MAND OG
KINDE by Hans Reitzels Forlag A/S Copenhagen
First published in Great Britain by Calder and Boyars Ltd 1971
This revised edition published in Penguin Handbooks 1980

The drawings by John Holder on pp. 10, 18, 55, 66 and 92
are based on the photos by Gregers Nielsen included in the
original Danish edition of the book
John Holder's drawings on pp. 27, 29, and 35 are based on
illustrations supplied by kind permission of the Consumers
Association Contraceptive Supplement and used in the first
British edition of the book

Made and printed in Great Britain by
Richard Clay (The Chaucer Press) Ltd,
Bungay, Suffolk
Set in Intertype Lectura

Contents

Foreword

This book was written for older children and young adults. The first edition was published in Denmark in 1968. At that time the Pornography Act was still in force, so the book caused quite a stir and came close to being banned. Six months after publication, the Act was repealed – and the book legalized.

During the past eleven years the book has had very wide sales at home and abroad. The Danish edition has been continually updated and has reprinted eleven times. Translations have been published in nine foreign countries. The book has been introduced into Danish schools, and has been accepted by most Danish parents.

The book is written from the viewpoint that young people have a right to objective information on sex. I have tried to make this the sort of book I myself would have liked when I was young. It need not be read from beginning to end; you may well use it as a reference book, looking up the subjects that interest you in the Contents list or the index.

B. H. CLAËSSON
March 1979

Sexuality in children

Sexual instinct and sexual urges do not suddenly start at puberty.

We can already see how an infant's hand will often move quite involuntarily towards the sex organs – something, by the way, which can also be seen in adults who have just woken up, either after ordinary sleep or after an anaesthetic. The infant, then, will play with his or her sex organs simply for pleasure. Boys will frequently make their penis go stiff, and both boys and girls may tickle themselves so strenuously that they become quite red in the face.

While they are still very young, children become conscious of which sex they belong to – as boys or girls – and for some time they may be totally absorbed in the interesting question of where the difference between the two lies. They compare themselves to adults, discover that one day they are going to be just like mummy or daddy; but there the comparison remains – impertinent and inquisitive. On investigation, children realize how nice it is to be tickled 'on the bottom' – and by someone else. Even so, their games are never protracted, as they so often are in later childhood, though there is no doubt that young children can be sexually attracted and express their feelings for one another.

Many young children will have phases of walking round fiddling quite openly with their sex organs. Usually this is just a pleasurable activity, like thumb-sucking, but frequent fiddling, just like continuous thumb-sucking, may be a sign that something is wrong with the child's relationship with his parents, family and friends.

School children, from the age of seven until puberty, may be deeply interested in each other. They sometimes talk about emotional, childish infatuations and want to go to bed with one another.

Many games, moreover, may have a sexual quality: doctors and nurses, for example. Here the intention is obviously to create a play-situation in which the children are *allowed* to see and feel each other's sex organs.

Adults react very differently to the sexual play of children. It is, however, being recognized that sexuality plays an important and natural part in a child's life. It is one of the many ways in which

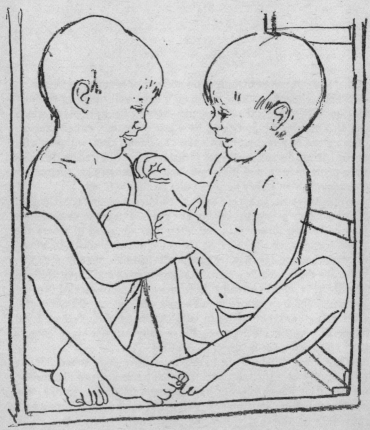

Erotic play between small children.

children prepare themselves for adult life. A warm and open attitude on the part of parents and elder brothers and sisters towards the child's interest and pleasure in sexual play can therefore play a large part in determining the child's later sexual and emotional development.

Puberty
and the years
that follow

Puberty is the name given to that period of our lives, lasting several years, when we cross the bridge from childhood to the adult world. The physical and mental changes taking place inside you may seem so total that after a few years it is hard to recognize yourself, just as other people may fall about in astonishment that it really is little Peter or Jane who has changed *so* much.

Early or late development

There is a wide variety in the ages at which individual people reach puberty.

On average girls are sexually mature a year or so earlier than boys. Thus for girls puberty starts at around 11–13 years, as opposed to boys, for whom puberty does not begin until they are 12–14 years old. In a small minority of girls the first signs of puberty may even be noticeable as early as 9 years old, or conversely as late as 17. Similarly there may be great variations in the ages at which boys enter the first phases of puberty, from 11 to 18 years old.

If puberty starts early and is accompanied by considerable growth, you will also stop growing earlier – on average it is 4–6 years from the beginning of puberty to full height. Hereditary conditions determine how tall or short you are in the end, just as the time at which puberty starts is also supposed to be a question of heredity. Good, varied food is a necessity if you are to grow to your full potential. It is the improved diet of the average young person in the wealthier countries today, together with extra vitamins, which is chiefly responsible for his or her being taller and more sexually mature at a slightly earlier age than young people were a hundred years ago.

Physical changes

At the beginning of puberty, the arms, legs, neck, trunk and sex organs all start to grow. Growth can take place either gradually or in leaps and bounds, and only rarely affects the whole body equally. On the contrary, the arms, legs and neck usually grow faster than the trunk, and boys especially can become so bony and lanky that it is hard to find clothes to fit them – and parents may be reluctant to pay very much for their clothes because they know that it will not be long before their children have grown out of them.

Girls' figures become more rounded, as a layer of fat settles under the skin. The pelvis grows and widens, so that it can later function as a channel during birth.

Both boys' and girls' voices break. Boys may take some time to find their bass pitch and their voices may break easily, especially when they are shouting (though this may be embarrassing at the time, this stage won't last long). Girls' voices also become a little deeper, acquiring more fullness and tone. These changes are due to the growth of the vocal cords and the larynx. This is more evident in boys, in whom the projection of the larynx on the neck is called the adam's apple.

When the muscles and bones develop in boys, they want to try out their new strength. They may begin to get a growth of beard, and for some this can present a real problem. Should they begin to shave? On the one hand they may be shy about their downy faces, hoping that no one has noticed, while on the other hand they are secretly proud of this sign of virility.

Some girls may also get a slight growth of hair on the face. It is usually very fine and light and best left alone; some people feel embarrassed about it, but the chances are that nobody notices it but you, and if you remove it, it will probably grow back thicker.

However, if it is making you miserable you should seek medical advice about safe methods of removal.

The most absorbing aspect of physical change in puberty can be the growth of the sex organs, disturbing on one hand, but very exciting on the other. In boys, the penis grows larger and thicker and darker-skinned (in light-skinned men), and strange new sensations can be felt in it. It is gradually assuming the characteristics of what is also a fertilizing organ. The scrotum and the balls grow at the same time and the scrotum becomes darker in colour. Internally, the prostate gland, the spermatic cord and the seminal vesicles also grow.

The sex organs of girls develop towards their mature form in the same way. The breasts grow and the nipples become larger and darker. Often one breast develops more quickly than the other. The clitoris and the labia also become larger. In some girls the inner labia may become visible between the outer. Internally the vagina, the womb, the fallopian tubes and the ovaries are all developing (see pp. 26–30). Some boys may also experience some minor development of the breasts, but this always disappears again quickly, so you need not be worried or embarrassed by it.

Both boys and girls are often worried that they are not developing 'normally'. In fact 'normal' is a rather misleading word because we are all built very differently and development takes place at different rates for different people. A girl who is teased for being 'flat' one year may be a completely different shape the next, whereas some girls grow quite large breasts to start with and they decrease in size over the next few years. In fact the size of your breasts or penis makes no difference to your ability to be sexually satisfied and satisfying. Nor, incidentally, does the size of your breasts affect your ability to suckle a baby.

For both boys and girls prevailing fashions in body shape can cause misery. If we look at British or American films of twenty or so years ago we can see that the fashion then was for men to be broadshouldered and tough-looking, whereas the image in the sixties and later favoured slimly built men. Clothes fashions changed accordingly from padded shoulders to slimline fitted jackets and tight trousers. Fashion in female shapes varies even more radically from year to year. Clearly no one can change their body to suit the trends, so unless you are grossly over- or under-weight there really isn't any need to be concerned. Besides, if you can convince yourself that your body is beautiful you will be surprised to find how many people agree with you!

As her breasts grow, a girl will usually consider whether to begin wearing a bra. It can be uncomfortable to have 'flapping' breasts when you run; it may even be painful. In this case a bra will help, but it shouldn't be too tight or the breasts will not be able to grow freely. There is no particular reason to start wearing a bra if you feel comfortable without one.

In both sexes hair appears under the arms and around the sex organs. In boys, particularly, hair grows on various other parts of the body, though this varies from a sprinkling of hair on the chest to a thick growth over chest, stomach and shoulders. In addition, the composition of one's sweat changes, the tendency to sweat becomes more pronounced, and thus body odour becomes more powerful (see p. 128). The skin and hair begin to get greasy and many young people develop blackheads and pimples. Probably the only positive thing that can be said about spots is that they *will* go away as you get older. In the meantime, don't curl up with shame and see your complexion as a personal affliction. It is one you share with most young people and, just as you would not reject another person because of their spots, there is no reason why they should reject you because of yours. For advice on controlling pimples, see pp. 127–8.

Sexual maturity

When a girl has her first period and a boy his first ejaculation we say that they have reached sexual maturity. Exactly what this means is explained in the next chapter on the sex organs. They are, however, signs that a girl can have children and a boy can make a girl pregnant.

For boys, sexual maturity means that the semen is emptied out at more or less regular intervals. This may happen either involuntarily, most often during sleep, or voluntarily as a result of masturbation, petting or intercourse.

Wet dreams (involuntary, nocturnal ejaculation) may be erotic. The first time it happens wet dreams may seem like the bed-wetting dream of a child, but they soon acquire a more sexual content.

Some boys may be worried because they leave tell-tale marks

on pyjamas and bedclothes. But this is nothing to be ashamed about. Wet dreams are quite natural – and your parents know this.

Although the sperm is being continually produced inside the body, wet dreams will decrease or disappear altogether, depending on how often you masturbate.

If you are absolutely determined to hide this particular sign of puberty from your parents, you can always masturbate before bed-time or go to bed with your underpants on, since they are usually quite a bit tighter than pyjama trousers and therefore more likely to absorb the sperm so that none leaks out and stains the sheets.

At about this time, you may become aware of unexpected erections which may not be connected with a sexual situation. It is common for men to have 'involuntary' erections when they are afraid or embarrassed. The apparent inappropriateness of this response may make you feel even more afraid or embarrassed. Unless you are wearing swimming trunks (in which case a quick cold plunge will soon solve the problem) or something similar, it is unlikely to be very noticeable to anyone else, and the erection will disappear as the situation changes and you feel more relaxed. The best advice is to try to ignore it (see also p. 36). It is perhaps ironic that erections in public are so embarrassing, whereas in private they are often considered more important than any other aspect of sex!

As we have said, maturity in girls is indicated physically by the first period. Your first period should be a positive and important sign of approaching adulthood. Sadly, periods have become associated in many people's minds with superstitions and sexual guilt. According to some religions, women are actually considered 'unclean' during this perfectly natural phase of their menstrual cycles. In fact, some adults feel so confused about their attitudes to periods that they don't tell their daughters what is going to happen, and the unexplained bleeding can be very frightening. If you feel concerned, or unclear about what is happening to you at this time, it helps to talk about it with friends or relations. Your periods will come every month between puberty and menopause (around the age of fifty) if you are not pregnant or ill, so it helps to come to terms with them early on. If you are having physical problems such as pain or heavy bleeding, see p. 129 for advice.

Around the time of your first period you may well experience faintness or weakness because of all the changes going on inside you. If you are bleeding heavily, you could well become short of iron, which is important for keeping you alert and healthy. It is sensible to eat 'iron-right' foods at this time, such as green leafy vegetables and liver. If you feel weak, weepy and dizzy for any length of time you should go to your doctor. He can test your blood for iron and if necessary prescribe iron pills.

On the more cheerful side, it is quite likely that you will have started to have sexual fantasies, dreams and erotic feelings. These are not directly connected to your period; they may come at any time and are a sign that your mind is also preparing itself for sexual experience.

Emotional changes

During the teens, an unbelievable amount of psychological changes are taking place. The adult world is opening out before you and a number of things you have never even dreamed of suddenly become full of meaning. On the one hand you are conscious of disturbing signals from your growing body, and on the other you are perceiving and adjusting to the people around you, who also seem changed, both because you are looking at them with new eyes and because adults really are changing their attitude towards you.

You may fall in love for the first time, and while the feeling lasts you may find it impossible to think about anything else. The other person will be in your thoughts day and night and you may feel such an overwhelming desire to be with him or her that you will put everything else aside to meet this need.

It might also happen that the person to whom you feel so strongly attracted doesn't even seem to notice that you exist, and your life will revolve around trying to bump into the object of your love 'accidentally'. Sooner or later you will find someone who responds to your feelings, but there is a risk even then that there will come a day when the relationship is broken off and you feel as if you will never be happy again. Life may seem to have lost all meaning for you. But luckily the self-preservation instinct wins through and after a while the whole thing will be forgotten – well, nearly, because such a powerful experience leaves its mark on the memory.

At other times your imagination and intellect become totally caught up in all sorts of new problems, theoretical and practical. There is also the discovery that you are a member of a society which imposes its own particular demands. Suddenly you have to decide what attitude you are going to adopt towards education and work, while life at school makes greater demands on your mind. At first some young people find all these things so overpowering and confusing that they may try to prolong the secure refuge of childhood by concealing from the people around them the signs that they are entering adulthood.

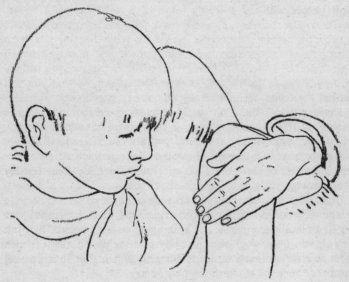

It is hard to think about anything else when you're in love.

It is hard to be the odd one out

Friends play a fantastically important part in the growth to maturity, and for this reason it can be very hard to be either an early or a late developer.

Early developers may come in for some teasing from the rest of their class, though this is basically due to envy. It can be even worse

18

to feel that you are the smallest – a child among the grown-ups. The kind of teasing you are subjected to then can become so intolerable that it might be an idea to find some way of changing your group of friends so that you have a chance to achieve a better position in a new circle of people.

Finding your real self

Most people will feel a strong sense of involvement with a particular crowd of friends, and this group will be of great significance in the later development of the individual. While beginning to form some opinions about who and what you are, you may well attach a great deal of importance to what your friends think of you and try to copy them, both in appearance and behaviour, so that you will not be considered different or thrown out of the group.

These considerations obviously play an important part in the formation of different attitudes and responses to sexual matters. If you belong to a group of friends in which the others have already had some sexual experience, or say they have, it immediately seems very important that you should try yourself – even if you are terribly unsure and possibly do not even want to yet.

Quite often you may have to join another group of people, because you have moved, perhaps, changed schools, left school, changed your job or been abandoned by the group you were in before. But you may also decide of your own free will to change your circle of friends because you find that your ideas differ from theirs on an increasing number of topics – of which sex may be one.

Changing groups voluntarily because you no longer find any satisfaction in belonging, or being thrown out of a group because the others cannot accept your views on some subject or another are signs that you are beginning to find your own way in the world.

Possibly, in private, you will stand in front of a mirror 'posing', in order to find out who you really are. You may be so spellbound by a film star, a pop idol, an adult, an older brother or sister, or a friend you admire that you practise being as like them as you can, imitating voice, gestures, facial expressions, clothes and so on.

After a while the role you are playing (the 'clown', the 'dope', the 'dumb blonde') may feel identical to your own personality, until eventually you grow tired of it because you realize that it did not totally express what you really are.

You may change roles several times; this is often a necessary part of trying to pinpoint what your true self is.

Obviously the roles you have most success with will be the most difficult to drop – even if they only reflect a minor part of your character and potential. This kind of clinging to security is undoubtedly one of the chief reasons why many adults remain dependent throughout their lives on the role which they think makes them most popular and which ties them most strongly to the group they find most attractive.

You may feel more secure acting in the way your friends expect you to behave. But your life will be very much more varied and exciting if you remain open to new ideas and feel free to reject those which you feel unhappy about. If you allow your attitudes to become rigid and fixed, you will find that in time they grow into unshakeable prejudices, and prejudice not only holds back your own development as a human being; on a larger scale, it also holds back the development of a more liberal and equitable society.

Once you have reached your twenties, therefore, both for your own sake and the sake of society, you ought to try to determine how many of the attitudes shared by your group of friends are also basically your own. At the same time you should make up your mind whether you are prepared to suppress your changing attitudes and ideas in order to tie yourself to any one particular, biased role, which it may be impossible to discard once you have been playing it for ten or twenty years.

Scruples of this kind may also lead individual, more mentally mature, teenagers to break with their friends and stop playing roles in an attempt to be themselves – for good or ill.

Problems with parents

In most societies parents are deeply interested in their children's transition from the world of the child to that of the adult, of which they themselves are after all the closest representatives. It is thus quite common for them to protect their child from the sort of information or experiences which would admit the child to an adult 'mystery' – particularly of a sexual nature.

At various times during your teens, at birthdays for example, adults may tell you that you are getting to be a real grown-up, but they rarely mean what they say. In any case, it is only in exceptional cases that you will see them accepting the consequences of their words.

Young people half-way through puberty may not necessarily feel particularly grown-up. Yet the increasing development of consciousness and the strange transformations taking place in the body point the way to adult life. So, for some of them, it becomes important to act more grown-up than they really are. This boosts self-confidence but also creates many problems. They start consciously asserting their new-found independence – often adopting the opinions of friends or adults they admire.

Through your new – adult – eyes, you can see more and more clearly that the adult world is not all that perfect; it is full of prejudice and narrow-minded rules. And this sharpens your sense of criticism, so that you soon find yourself in conflict with your parents, among others. What you may find it hard to realize is that many grown-ups are also unhappy, insecure and disappointed people, who can only cope with life by maintaining the traditional parental position of authority, upholding futile rules and a façade of idyllic perfection in front of their children because of their own fears.

Many parents of course feel justifiable concern for their children's welfare. They may have had bitter experiences themselves and can hardly bear to see their children repeating their own mistakes. But experience is not always something that can be read about or dictated; it is something only very gradually acquired.

Many women who are tied to the home, and parents who have lost their partners through death or divorce find that life suddenly seems to have lost its purpose. So they cling to their adolescent children, restricting their freedom and rights – or falling into self-pity and 'illness' which indirectly tie the children to them.

Other parents may become thoroughly jealous – they can see their children living an apparently irresponsible, free and easy life that they never knew when they were children. Everyone knows the expression 'Now, when I was young . . .'

Whatever the reason, relations between parents and teenage children are often intolerable. The economic dependence which our society imposes on young people, and which can be as much of a strain for parents as for children, only increases the difficulties. Many of you may have had remarks like 'You're treating home more and more like a hotel' flung at you by an infuriated father or mother; and they may be both right and wrong.

Parents could do a great deal themselves to improve the kind of contact they have with their children, above all by being more fair-minded, making allowances for mistakes and uncertainties, and including young people in their adult lives as instructively as they can, without any petty moralizing. And young people, on their side, could try to put themselves in their parents' position a bit more, making an effort to see them as people with good and bad points.

Even with good will on both sides, agonizing moments of conflict can arise, but these encounters contribute towards making the young into detached and independent people. They are a necessary stage in the process of mental and emotional development.

Youth and society

In the animal kingdom, animals begin to reproduce as soon as they reach sexual maturity. It is important for the survival of the species. Among humans also, there was a time when sexual maturity meant the beginning of sexual behaviour and reproduction. In some cultures still, boys and girls are married at puberty.

In Britain, both partners have to be eighteen before they can get married without their parents' permission, and to obtain permission they must be over sixteen. It is forbidden by law to have intercourse with someone who is under the age of sixteen – the 'age of consent'. For homosexual men, the age of consent has been set at twenty-one. There is no specific law on 'legal age' for lesbian women.

These regulations show quite clearly how society has changed its attitudes so that it is no longer considered desirable for sexual maturity to be the natural start of sexual experience and its consequences. These laws are intended partly to protect the young against the burden of parenthood before they are ready for it and to prevent the birth of too many children into what could be an emotionally insecure and financially unstable environment. They are also intended as a protection for young people against sexual exploitation by adults. However, these laws are also an expression of prejudice against certain forms of sexual expression, and they can be repressive to those people who do not fit society's standard patterns.

This 'protective' attitude has developed because an industrialized society has an increasing need for its citizens to be educated to perform certain tasks, and while we are learning those tasks we are unlikely to have enough money to support our children adequately. But during this learning time, our sexual desires do not go away.

In the chapter on masturbation we mention that almost all boys and girls masturbate during this time. This form of release may be satisfying on its own for some years, but there comes a time, which varies from person to person, when most people want to share these sexual feelings with someone else. You will always find adults who don't want you to. They think you are too young and should wait either until you are married or at least until you are well and truly engaged, since an engagement is seen by most people as being as binding as marriage. Then if anything goes wrong, you can be quickly piloted into marriage.

For many young people the decision to enter into a sexual relationship may be difficult – sometimes because they feel genuinely unready for it, or possibly because they are afraid of condemnation from parents or friends. It may be that moral attitudes instilled into them from an early age are unshakeable, or produce such feelings of guilt that sex becomes something to fear. For young homosexual men and women the fear of being 'found out' is even more acute. In many families the possibility of loving a member of one's own sex may never have been mentioned, and it is likely that any references to homosexuality they have heard either at home or elsewhere will have been derogatory or pitying. In this atmosphere it is hardly surprising that early relationships will often be fraught with guilt and fear. It would be misleading to suggest that this unease is wholly unfounded, but there are a number of organizations (listed on pp. 135–6) which will give you the opportunity to discuss your feelings with others. With support you will find it much easier to be open about your relationships and to convince yourself and your friends that homosexuality is nothing to be ashamed of. (See pp. 45–7 for more on this subject.)

For other young people, one of the biggest inhibitors is fear of pregnancy. The problem is always greatest for girls, because not only do the consequences of an unwanted pregnancy fall mainly on their shoulders but they are also victims of a double standard of morality: young men may 'sow their wild oats' but a young woman who does the same sort of thing may be branded as 'easy' or a 'tart'. Clearly nowadays such attitudes are as illogical as they are unfair. They are just one aspect of the continuing inequality of the sexes.

In the past, while women had little chance of supporting themselves or their children, and sex almost inevitably led to pregnancy, chastity was the price they had to pay for the economic security of marriage. A woman was part of her husband's assets. She cooked, cleaned, spun, sewed, bore children and reared them in return for that security. Gradually this contract which was based on women's inequality and dependence was strengthened by a mythology in which women were told that they had no sexual feelings and that if they did they were wicked. Sex they were told is a male weakness and if women played their cards right they could use that weakness to land themselves a rich or handsome husband.

But attitudes to sex gradually started to change, and in the sixties mass contraception heralded the dawn of what became known as the 'permissive' society. Some girls and women who in the past would have exchanged only the odd kiss and cuddle for a night out, saving the 'real thing' to exchange for a wedding ring, now felt that they should go 'all the way' in return for the odd half at the pub and a little attention. They were still regarding sex as a commodity for exchange, but the exchange rate had gone down!

Widely publicized research into female sexuality has now shown that women do of course have strong sexual feelings and an enormous capacity for sexual pleasure as long as they and their sexual partners have learned how their bodies work. Many women discover that for themselves without reading text books about it; others, who may have more subtle sexual responses, have learned not to expect pleasure and so they shut their minds off and repress their feelings.

This confusion of expectation and needs means that for many girls a boyfriend is considered not so much a friend as a symbol of belonging in a society that only acknowledges people in pairs. Fear of losing this symbol means that it is as difficult as ever for a young woman to make decisions about sex based on her own needs rather than on fears of losing her boyfriend or of losing his respect. But, if girls stop to think about it, they need not go on using sex as an exchange, because now it is easier to pay their own way. For the first time they can enjoy sex without fear of pregnancy, when they want to – and say no when they do not. The ability to say *no*, and mean it, is just as much a sign of sexual maturity and independence as the ability to say yes, or even to do the asking when it feels right.

How soon do others go to bed with each other – and why?

Investigations have shown that nearly all young people think that their friends have had more sexual experience than they have. What little statistical evidence there is about sexual experience among young people is not very reliable, but it varies according to social class, relationships with parents and length of education. Young people who get on well with their parents and/or spend longer in the education system tend to start sexual relationships later than those who get on badly with their parents and leave school early. Obviously, between the two extremes there exist endless combinations. Research also shows that few people under the age of sixteen have experienced intercourse.

Little is also known about the reasons why young people first have sexual intercourse. Admitting that such classifications are over-simplified, however, it is probably true to say that about half of all young men and a higher proportion of girls first have intercourse because they feel emotionally involved with their partner. Information from family planning clinics indicates that the majority of young women seeking contraceptive advice for the first time are involved in stable relationships.

Some people have intercourse for the first time out of curiosity; the younger they are at the time of their first experience, the more likely it is that they were prompted by curiosity.

The female sex organs

The female sex organs are divided into the outer organs, which can be seen from outside, and the inner organs, which are hidden in the lower half of the abdomen.

The outer sex organs

We include here the labia majora and minora, the hymen (maidenhead), the clitoris and the mons veneris (the pubic bone, which is covered by hair). One can also regard the breasts as outer organs.

The hymen is a little crease of membrane which partly covers the entrance to the vagina. It usually breaks during a girl's first intercourse, though it may also happen during petting or if she uses internal tampons during menstruation. Breaking the hymen can cause a certain amount of soreness and bleeding, but if you read the section on intercourse (p. 65) you will see that there are ways in which this can be minimized. Very few girls experience the sort of pain that some romantic fiction writers are so fond of dwelling on.

The entrance to the vagina is surrounded by the labia minora, which end in front of the clitoris, and these labia minora are partly covered by the labia majora, which are carried right out into the mons veneris. Behind the clitoris lies the opening to the urethra, and below the entrance to the vagina is the anus (see the diagram opposite). The clitoris, or more accurately to the of the clitoris, is the

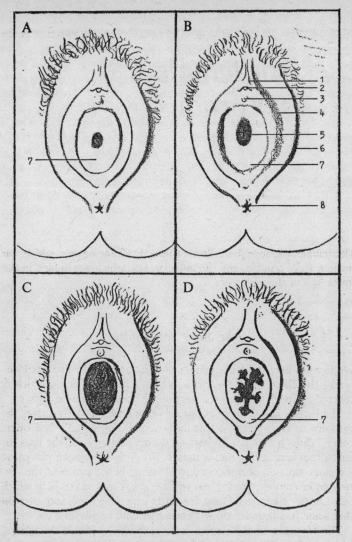

Figures A, B, C and D show the different shapes the hymen may take. 1. The body of the clitoris. 2. The tip of the clitoris. 3. The opening of the urethra. 4. The labia minora. 5. The opening of the vagina. 6. The labia majora. 7. The hymen. 8. The anus.

In figure C the hymen is so small and the opening of the vagina so large that a tampon can be used without any difficulty.

most sensitive part of the woman; it is as responsive to touch as the tip of the penis is, and is therefore also the most important organ of love-making both before and during intercourse. In fact some women find that their clitoris is so sensitive that direct touch is painful and they prefer to be touched above or around this area rather than directly on the clitoris.

The size of both the clitoris and the labia minora may vary greatly from one girl to another, just as the right and left labia are rarely the same size. These differences have no importance as far as sexual relations are concerned, though right in the beginning it may be more awkward to find a small clitoris than a large one.

Between the labia a whitish, waxy secretion is produced. It has a distinct aroma which both women and men usually find arousing.

The breasts

Development of the breasts is one of the signs that a girl has reached puberty.

As you know, the breast has two functions. One is the suckling of children; soon after birth the breasts start producing milk to feed the baby. The other function is a sexual one. The breasts, particularly the nipples, are among the most sexually sensitive parts of a woman, and the sight and feel of naked breasts also stimulate a strong sexual response in others.

Boys should remember that the breasts are sensitive and may hurt if they are treated roughly. Just before a period they sometimes swell and become so sensitive that they are almost untouchable.

The inner sex organs

These include the vagina, the womb, the fallopian tubes and the ovaries.

The vagina is a cleft, 7–10 centimetres long (3½–4 inches), with very elastic walls which can be widely stretched, as they have to be during childbirth. The walls of the vagina are covered with a fluted,

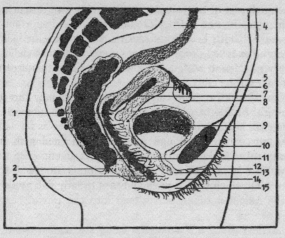

Above: The female internal sex organs dissected lengthways. 1. The mouth of the womb. 2. The anus. 3. The vagina. 4. The rectum. 5. The left fallopian tube. 6. The womb. 7. The cavity of the womb. 8. The left ovary. 9. The bladder. 10. The pubic bone. 11. The rectum. 12. The clitoris. 13. The opening of the urethra. 14. The labia minora. 15. The labia majora.

Below: The female internal sex organs dissected across. 1. The two ovaries: the one on the left of the picture has been dissected. 2. The two fallopian tubes: the one on the left of the picture has been dissected. 3. The cavity of the womb. 4. The womb. 5. The mouth of the womb. 6. The vagina, dissected and opened out; note the ribbed membrane.

mucous membrane (like a washboard); during intercourse the un-evenness intensifies the sensations in the man.

The womb, which is shaped remarkably like a pear, joins the vagina at the end. This 'pear' is turned on its head with the thinnest part, 'the stalk', protruding a little way down into the vagina. This stalk is called the cervix and is hollow, so that a tiny passage, the cervical canal, leads up into the interior of the womb. The cervical canal is very narrow, so you need have no fear that a tampon or any-thing else will be able to disappear up it.

The womb, or uterus, is also hollow and is lined with mucous membrane to which a fertilized egg attaches itself; once there it develops links with the blood vessels on the walls of the womb and grows into an embryo. The egg reaches the womb by way of two ducts, the fallopian tubes, which lead into the top of the womb from the ovaries.

The ovaries, which are about the same size as a walnut, lie on each side of the abdomen (see diagram on p. 29). They produce hormones and eggs. These hormones are chemical substances which affect, among other things, the monthly bleeding and the ability of the womb to keep the fertilized egg firmly lodged inside it. The ovaries also act as a store for the eggs. In sexually mature women, one egg is released from one of the ovaries every twenty-six to thirty days (usually midway between the start of one period and the next), a process known as ovulation, and is then carried along its fallopian tube down into the cavity of the womb. Incidentally ovulation may cause a slight ache at the bottom of either the right or left side of the abdomen.

Fertilization

During intercourse the man squirts out his semen into the end of the vagina. His sperm cells are mobile and travel up through the cervical canal, on through the womb, and up into both fallopian tubes. If these cells encounter an egg, a single cell will burrow its way into the egg and it is then said that fertilization has taken place. The fertilized egg then travels down the tube and becomes lodged in the mucous membrane which forms the lining of the womb. The woman is now pregnant, and the period of nine months during which the foetus develops into a baby capable of surviving on its own is called a pregnancy.

Twins

If the fertilized egg divides into two at an early stage, each half can develop into a separate foetus. This causes what we call one-egg or identical twins. In some women two mature eggs are released at the same time and if both are fertilized and then become lodged in the womb they will develop into two foetuses. This causes two-egg twins, who are not identical in looks.

Menstruation

If the egg is not fertilized, it will travel down into the vagina and slip out unnoticed. In the meantime the membrane of the lining of the womb will have grown thick and rich in food content ready for the fertilized egg. If the egg is not fertilized this membrane comes away from the wall of the womb. As the membrane is shed a few of the small blood vessels in the womb break, but there is much less bleeding than you may think and what comes away is membrane dyed by blood. This flows down into the vagina and out of it. The process is known as menstruation ('monthly period', 'the curse') and may last for between three and nine days, though usually between four and six days.

When menstruation is finished the membrane begins to grow again, and about fourteen days before the first day of the next period a new egg is released from the ovaries. So from one menstruation to the next there is usually an interval of between twenty-six and thirty days. It continues in the same way for an average of thirty-five years, from between the ages of twelve to thirteen (nine to seventeen at the extreme) until a woman reaches forty to fifty-five and enters the change of life or menopause.

Quite often women have a certain amount of bother with menstruation. It may be irregular and it can cause pain in the abdomen. Although these troubles are not usually connected with disease of any kind, for practical reasons they are dealt with in the chapter on disease and other problems (pp. 129–30).

The most usual way of dealing with the blood is by using either sanitary towels or tampons. Towels are sold in packets; some have to be worn with a belt which must be bought separately; others come with special pants which they fit into; and still others can be attached to your own pants. These days most towels are 'disposable', though if too many of them are put down the toilet they tend to block up the drains. Most public lavatories provide disposal bins to put them in.

Tampons are put inside the vagina, where they absorb the blood. Many women prefer this internal protection because a tampon usually can't be felt once in place, and it cannot slip when you are doing sports or dancing. It is possible that if you are still a virgin a tampon may be difficult to remove because it swells slightly. You may break your hymen while trying to get it out, but that is certainly nothing to worry about. If the tampon seems to be hopelessly stuck it can be removed by a doctor or at a clinic, but this is extremely unlikely to happen; if you use your muscles (bearing down as if you were moving your bowels) you can probably reach in and haul it out with a finger. It is most important not to leave a tampon inside you at the end of your period as this can cause infection.

Some women find that tampons and towels are rather expensive and use either their diaphragms (see p. 68) or small natural sponges with a string attached which can be washed out in cold water and reinserted, though this is not a good idea if you have an infection.

Whatever kind of protection you use, be sure to change or wash it frequently; the stronger the bleeding the more often you will need to change, sometimes several times a day.

Hygiene

The walls of your vagina are kept clean by your own secretions, so there is never any need to wash inside. However, once the secretions, or the blood at period time, drip outside they begin, after a while, to decay and smell. This can cause mild infections of the vagina and may irritate your vulva. Because people are not always aware of their own smells you may not realize that this is happening, so it is best to wash yourself regularly to be sure. All you need to use is mild soap and water. Vaginal deodorants are never necessary, and they may cause irritation.

Don't, however, expect to wash all your smell away. We all have our own unique smell, which should be quite pleasant. If it is unpleasant or different from usual, you may have an infection (see p. 130).

The male sex organs

The man's sex organs consist of the penis, the scrotum, which holds the two balls or testicles, two epididymises, two seminal ducts (vas deferens), two seminal vesicles, the prostate gland and the urethra.

The penis is composed of spongy tissue. The top part is called the head or gland; the rest is called the body or shaft. The head of the penis is the most sensitive part of the man, as sensitive as the woman's clitoris. Usually the head is covered by a thick fold of skin, the foreskin, which can be drawn right back. (For tightness of the foreskin, see p. 134.) Under the foreskin, an odorous, whitish waxy secretion, called smegma, is produced.

The scrotum and the balls

The scrotum is a bag of thin skin with a scattered growth of hair. Inside it is divided into two compartments, each one containing one ball. When exposed to the cold the scrotum shrinks, a phenomenon which can also be observed during powerful sexual excitement.

The balls are the size of small plums, firm and smooth. They are not always exactly the same size, and the left one usually hangs a little lower than the right. They slip between the fingers (like marbles in your pocket) but are highly sensitive to pressure or being hit. It is important for girls to remember this so that they do not squeeze them too hard when they are sexually stimulated.

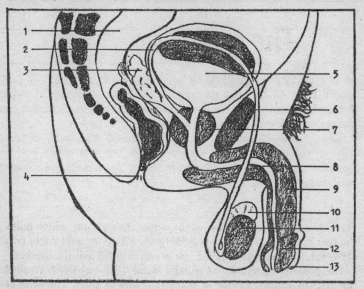

The male sex organs dissected lengthways. 1. The rectum. 2. The right spermatic duct. 3. The right seminal vesicle. 4. The anus. 5. The bladder. 6 The pubic bone. 7. The prostate gland. 8. The urethra. 9. Spongy tissue in the body of the penis. 10. The left epididymis. 11. The left testicle. 12. Spongy tissue in the head of the penis. 13. The foreskin.

The balls produce both hormones and sperm cells. Production continues throughout the day and night, regardless of whether the man is sexually active or not. The sperm cells are then stored in the epididymis, which lies outside the balls. Two pipes, the thickness of string, the seminal ducts, lead from the epididymis up into the abdomen and end in the prostate gland. The two seminal vesicles are lodged just behind the prostate gland and lead out into the seminal ducts. The sperm cells are carried along the ducts and into the seminal vesicles, where they are mixed with seminal fluid, which is produced in the prostate gland. This fluid is necessary for the mobility of the sperm cells. The finished semen is then pumped along the urethra, which runs through the prostate gland, and is finally squirted out through the opening of the urethra on the head of the penis. This process is called ejaculation.

Semen

Semen is a milky, slimy, sticky liquid with an insipid, slightly fishy smell. It is a little salty to the taste, with an aftertaste of vague bitterness. Semen is sterile (bacteria-free). It stains material but can be washed off with cold water and soap.

About a teaspoonful of semen is released with each orgasm, though the more frequent the ejaculation the less semen will be passed on each time. This amount of semen contains several hundred million sperm cells.

Erection

When the spongy tissue in the penis is filled with blood, it becomes longer, thicker and firmer until it finally stands erect. This is called an erection, a 'hard on' or a 'stiff prick'. Erection is usually due to some kind of erotic influence, though it can also be the result of other than immediately sexual causes. In puberty, especially, it can happen after very little irritation. The vibrations of some form of transport, for example, stomach exercises on a gym floor, even just the fear that it may happen, can cause the penis to stand revealingly away from the body. You may find this situation distressing and feel terribly embarrassed because you are not in control of what is happening. The best thing to do is concentrate on something completely different, or to tense the stomach muscles to breaking point. but if nothing helps you can always go and masturbate in the toilet.

Another cause of involuntary erection is dreaming. Both aggressive and erotic dreams can produce an erection, though only sexual dreams will also lead to ejaculation. Waking up in the morning with a hard-on is thus due to the content of your dreams and not – as was believed until recently – to a full bladder.

Big or small

There are countless misapprehensions as to the size of the penis. One of the things which keep these misunderstandings alive is that section of pornographic literature in which heavy-breasted women are described as being in hot pursuit of bigger and bigger pricks. But these books are mostly written by men, not women, and have very little to do with erotic reality. Although there can be great variations in the size of the limp penis from man to man, research has shown that these differences in size even out quite a bit with erection; so that what may seem a small penis when limp will become proportionately much larger when erect than one which appears large when limp. So any comparisons you try to draw with other people's penises will probably be unhelpful. In addition, fat men may be confused by the fact that part of the penis may be hidden in the fatty tissue around the pubic hair area.

Of course there will be differences – after all we are all built individually – but during intercourse these differences even out because a woman's vagina is sufficiently elastic to adapt to the size of a penis, big or small. For the same reason, she need have no fear that the penis will be too big for her vagina – there will always be room, unless the vagina is not sufficiently developed because the girl is not physically mature.

Hygiene

Although men are not so prone to genital infections as women are, it is still just as important to keep clean, if only to ensure that you do not infect your partner. Careful washing is particularly important if your penis is uncircumcised; you should carefully draw back the foreskin and wash underneath daily. The secretions that collect under the foreskin may cause a local infection, which will be irritating for you and is very easily transferred to the moist environment of a vagina.

Masturbation

Masturbation means manipulating the sexual organs with your hands, so the word can be used for something you do to someone else or yourself. It is also called onanism, a word stemming from the biblical story about Onan who was punished with death for refusing to give his dead brother children by impregnating his brother's widow. He interrupted intercourse with his sister-in-law by pulling out before ejaculation (the coitus interruptus method) and thus broke the prevailing law of the land.

The Christians of the Middle Ages were of the unhappy opinion that all sexual activity was sinful. So in order to frighten young people away from self-gratification, they altered the story and told them that Onan had been condemned to death by God for the sin of masturbation. Since then self-gratification has been called onanism.

In previous centuries the attitude to masturbation was hardly tolerant in Europe. In order to make young people feel guilty about it, books were written asserting that masturbation was a form of self-abuse which could lead to spinal consumption, brain fever and madness.

It goes without saying that these deliberate attempts to frighten have made life miserable for those countless people who continued to masturbate in spite of the terrifying prospects presented to them, making them anxious, ashamed, convinced of their own inferiority and full of self-reproach.

It is therefore hard to overestimate the importance of the fact that in recent years so many researchers into sexual matters have concerned themselves with this problem and are all agreed that masturbation is completely harmless.

Masturbation is very common

Research has shown that the majority of boys and young men masturbate from time to time, but it is not so widespread among young girls. About half of them masturbate as a form of release from sexual urges, and of those the majority begin either in connection with or following some other kind of sexual experience. It is reckoned that about three quarters of adult women have masturbated at one time or another.

These differences between the sexes have various causes. Firstly, boys and girls are differently brought up. Secondly, sexual maturity is indicated in different ways. Boys begin to experience involuntary nocturnal emission, which is accompanied by pleasurable sensations in the sex organs, whereas girls who begin to menstruate do not experience accompanying sexual feelings. Thirdly, the continuous production of semen in the balls gives rise to an underlying need for ejaculation. Finally, nature has made a boy's most sensitive part, the head of the penis, so accessible that it is continually exposed to irritation from clothes and fiddling from fingers, while a girl's most sensitive part, the clitoris, is protected by the labia. Thus boys very often discover at an early age how pleasant it can be to caress their own sex organs, while girls may take longer to find out how to duplicate for themselves the pleasant sensations they experience from, for example, the vibration of a moving train. Also girls are less likely to talk about it with their friends than boys are. This explains why many girls only begin to masturbate after some sexual experience.

It is quite harmless

Masturbation cannot lead to either mental or physical sickness. Nor can it, as some believe, deform the sex organs or prematurely exhaust them. The old myth that a man only produces a certain amount of semen in his life and therefore runs the risk of using up the supply unless he is careful has been shown to be nonsense. Similarly, there is absolutely no truth in the suggestion that you may later become impotent or frigid if you masturbate too much, though feelings of guilt about masturbation may mean that you experience such difficulties when you begin to have sex. But masturbation is not itself responsible for these problems. Some people blame masturbation because they feel tired or depressed or cannot keep up with their friends during sporting activities; but this is merely an exaggeration of ordinary experience following orgasm, when one may feel tired for about half an hour and need to gather one's strength again in the same way as one might after any demanding physical activity (a hundred-metre sprint, for example). If you feel tired and depressed for any longer than this interval then there must be other reasons – just as masturbation cannot affect your sporting performances unless you masturbate just before you are about to take part.

Although masturbation is harmless – just as not masturbating is harmless – some very shy and self-contained people who find great consolation in it may use it as a replacement for the emotional and sexual contacts they find it difficult to establish. Especially when you are a little older and masturbation has become a habit, you may have difficulty breaking out of your isolation. Similarly, some people may continue to masturbate when they are in a long-term relationship, not just because it is a pleasant thing to do but as a substitute every time any sexual difficulties arise, instead of tackling the problem together with their partner. In such cases it is not, however, masturbation itself which is at fault, but the way in which it is used.

When you are alone – by choice or because you don't have a sexual partner at the moment – masturbation is a pleasant way of releasing sexual tension and exploring your own sexual responses. For women in particular, masturbation can be more than a pleasant and comforting experience; it is a way of learning how your body works. Many women do not find it easy to have orgasms, and if they have experimented on their own they can then teach their partners how to do the things that work best for them.

How people masturbate

Boys usually masturbate by stroking or rubbing the penis or only the head of the penis rhythmically backwards and forwards between two fingers or in the hollow of the hand until orgasm is reached and the semen comes. Often this is done in such a way that the foreskin slides up and down over the head of the penis, unless the foreskin is too short for this technique. Girls usually masturbate by rubbing the clitoris or the surrounding area rhythmically with one or more fingers until sexual climax is achieved. For both sexes it varies as to whether they are firm or more careful and whether they prefer fast or slow movements – though usually the faster and firmer the movements the nearer one is to orgasm.

Some girls may have a series of orgasms at short intervals without their sexual excitement decreasing noticeably between them, whereas boys who have just had an orgasm are rarely able to achieve another immediately afterwards.

The realization that the technique may vary from person to person may be important when one first enters a sexual relationship. It is essential not to stick to one particular technique which one may have read about in a book but to make time to ask whether what one is doing is really what one's partner wants.

Variations in masturbation and masturbation fantasies

There is nothing particularly unusual in using aids to increase pleasure during masturbation. Boys may use all kinds of objects which feel good around their penises. Or they may like to take their clothes off, sometimes looking at themselves in a mirror. Girls may do comparable things. Both sexes may masturbate under running water in a shower, or may use mechanical aids such as electric massagers.

Masturbation is often accompanied by sexual fantasies. For certain people such fantasies will tend to repeat themselves, though they vary a great deal from person to person. Some may have realistic fantasies, based on some incident from real life which they have merely been prevented from putting into practice at the time; whereas others imagine more unrealistic situations. Some people may occasionally stimulate their fantasies with pornographic magazines. Masturbation fantasies are quite common and usually harmless, though, as we have mentioned earlier, there are those shy and solitary people who, apart from vivid masturbation fantasies, have a strong tendency to comforting but unrealistic daydreams. If you notice that you are doing this, try talking to an understanding friend, perhaps an older person.

Communal masturbation

More than half of all men have at some time during their teens or early twenties taken part in communal masturbation with other boys or young men. This consists either of masturbating each other or taking part in masturbation at the same time. There may be competitions about who, for example, can squirt his semen the furthest, who can 'toss himself off' the fastest or who can achieve a climax most often, together with many other variations. The possibilities are endless.

Girls may also have experience of communal masturbation, though this is not nearly so common as among boys.

Communal masturbation is a normal way of expressing your sexual impulses when you are young, and the sense of contact and fellow-feeling which may result in the group or between two partners can sometimes positively help sexual development. As soon as you have the opportunity to enter a more prolonged sexual relationship, the desire for communal masturbation will, as a rule, disappear of its own accord.

About love and being in love

Before passing on to descriptions of the more technical and physiological aspects of sexual life, I would like to say something about the emotional requirements which make a sexual relationship between two people successful.

You may go to bed with someone for a variety of reasons: because you are infatuated, in love, curious, worried about being different, anxious to please your partner, afraid of losing him or her, or just plain randy. And intercourse can be satisfying on a purely sensual level, regardless of the depth of feeling involved. Moral attitudes are irrelevant as a basis for judging the reasons for going to bed, still less for condemning them.

However, long experience has shown that when sexuality and emotions are totally separated, the sexual relationship may become less satisfactory for both partners.

But we need to be more precise about what kind of feelings are involved. You may feel great affection for your pets, your brothers and sisters, parents and friends. You may like playing with your dog though these feelings will have nothing to do with sex. The fact that you are capable, however, of feeling affection for other people and animals may provide a foundation on which to build permanent loving relationships later in life.

Infatuation

Especially when you are young, there are other, fiercer, emotions involved in the attraction between two people. We talk about falling in love or infatuation, and a strong infatuation can be an indescribable, almost ecstatic experience. The whole personality is involved in a feeling which pierces you right through. If the other person is also in love with you, you become immeasurably happy and everyone can see it. You walk more freely, your eyes shine more brightly, you feel very cheerful. All your good qualities blaze up just to please the person you have chosen – and to be encouraged by your friends and parents (unless the latter become anxious instead). But the strange thing about infatuation is that, even though the feeling may take hold of you in a matter of minutes, it can be so powerful that you regard it as a stroke of destiny. This experience becomes linked to all your ideas about 'the one and only', and you have the unshakeable feeling that you know him or her right to the depths of their being.

Obviously a state which can spring up so quickly need not necessarily have very much to do with the object of one's infatuation. It is above all a mental process which is provoked and maintained by the person one is in love with. In fact one is blind to everything except the things which have engendered the infatuation. After a time the other person's true personality is bound to emerge, and if you then find that they have many traits of character which you don't much care for, your infatuation will disappear, leaving a sad feeling of emptiness – or giving way to irritation, possibly even hate. Infatuation is subject to the harsh truth of the old saying 'easy come, easy go'.

'I love you' is an expression we whisper when we are in love – well, we feel the words inside even if we don't have the courage to say them. But it becomes an empty cliché when our infatuation fades and we still cling to the expression, as if to prove to ourselves and our partner that there is still something left of the old passion.

Although it is possible to experience such feelings in childhood, the infatuations of puberty are usually such an overwhelming experience that people have clear memories of them for the rest of their lives.

Homosexuality

Most young people find that puberty is also a time when they develop very strong and often quite emotional relationships with members of their own sex. A best friend is a support, confidant and partner in discovery. For some people relationships forged at this stage of their lives stay with them for ever, if not in reality, at least in memory. Almost everyone can remember back to a moment when their feelings of friendship spilled over into a desire for physical closeness, a need to touch. Sometimes these feelings will be worked out through playful fighting or teasing; sometimes they feel too powerful to express and you might withdraw guiltily or become awkward or tense. Sometimes the feelings are reciprocated and a friendship grows into something more complex.

Unfortunately, our society has tended to frown on sexual relationships between members of the same sex (homosexual), insisting that sex between men and women (heterosexual) is the only normal form of sexual expression. This rigid attitude is totally at odds with reality. Most people are capable of very strong feelings for members of their own sex as well as for members of the opposite sex but tend to conform to a heterosexual pattern by repressing or denying the other parts of the sexuality. Of course there are people at both ends of the sexual spectrum who have an aversion to sexual contact with people either of their own sex or the opposite sex, and there are people who are truly bisexual and enjoy sex with both men and women. All these different expressions of sexuality are equally valid, and are potentially equally pleasurable.

For those who are unable, or do not want, to conform to a heterosexual pattern, life can be hard. People who believe that sex should only be for having babies see homosexuals as extreme examples of people who indulge in 'sex for pleasure', and so they have been persecuted. Sometimes this persecution has been bolstered by misinformation, for example that homosexuals are 'child molesters'. There are of course adults, both homosexual and heterosexual, who are attracted to children (we discuss this on p. 116), but the vast majority of adult human beings want sex to be an aspect of a loving relationship with another adult. Homosexuals are no exception.

Persecution and prejudice have resulted in laws to 'curb' homosexual practices among men, for whom the age of consent (in England) is set at twenty-one. As homosexual acts are legal only in private, any public gesture of affection could be deemed illegal, even holding hands. Female homosexuality (lesbianism) is not illegal. It was left out of the laws curbing male homosexuals because Queen Victoria refused to believe that women (who were not supposed to be interested in sex at all) could do such a thing! Though safe from prosecution, lesbians suffer just as much from prejudice, so that they are effectively forced to hide their relationships from public view.

It is not surprising, given the degree of prejudice against homosexuality, that some young people feel ashamed and afraid when they feel drawn to members of their own sex. Some people transfer these feelings to members of the opposite sex; others pretend to do so in an attempt to convince themselves, and others, that they are 'normal'. These people may live heterosexual lives for years, marrying and even having families, either making do with the odd secret affair or refusing to admit, even to themselves, that they are unhappy and unfulfilled, sexually and emotionally.

Sex is an important part of our lives and it is sad that there should be some people who feel forced to repress their feelings. But attitudes are changing; increasingly homosexuals are refusing to hide their sexuality and live in the 'closet'. It is far easier to be openly homosexual now than it was even ten years ago. This might not seem much of a reassurance if you are fighting with feelings now that you don't know how to express. You may well feel afraid of rejection if you show your feelings openly. Adolescence for you may seem unendurably painful, but don't despair. You are not nearly as isolated as you feel; approximately one in every ten people are also homosexual so you are bound to meet people who feel as you do before long. There are a number of organizations which run social events for 'gay' people and provide sympathetic counselling as well. See pp. 135–6 for details.

Homosexuals will inevitably continue to feel vulnerable and isolated while everyone else continues to treat them as if they were potentially violent or somehow disgusting. If anything, homosexuals, far from being violent, are more tentative in their approach to other people; after all they have a much greater fear of rejection. And there is nothing at all mysterious about the ways in which homosexuals make love. All adults have roughly the same sexual equipment, and, as we describe in the section on making love (pp. 58–63), there are an infinite number of ways of giving each other pleasure which do not include heterosexual intercourse.

A few words about responsibility

One of the characteristics of puberty is that one's moods and emotions are very unstable. One day you feel on top of the world and full of self-confidence; the next you are down in the dumps, depressed, insecure and bewildered. If you are in a good mood you have a great deal of affection to spare for those you care for. If not, you hate everybody.

You may be very impressionable and your friends' opinions (or what you think their opinions are) may have a great influence on the way you behave. You may let the advice of adults, however sensible, go in one ear and out the other. It is essential for one's personal development that one gains mental and physical experience oneself.

Meanwhile there are certain kinds of activities which are bound to affect the lives of others or which may have incalculable consequences for one's own future so that it may be sensible to listen to an adult's advice to think seriously before one embarks on them. Sexual activities belong to this category.

Adolescent boys and girls are still on an unequal footing as regards sexual matters and this may take any number of years to change. Although both may form romantic attachments without bringing particular sexual desires to the relationship, most boys who have reached sexual maturity have experienced during masturbation the delight of orgasm and now feel a deep desire to reach a climax 'in the right way'. Meanwhile fewer girls will have experienced orgasm through masturbation, so that for them sexual feelings are not necessarily concentrated in the desire to experience intercourse and orgasm. This is not to say that girls do not experience sexual feelings. Most women have a much more diffused sexuality than men; they enjoy being stroked and caressed, and the part of sex which is often dismissed as a preliminary to the 'real thing' is for many girls the most important part of it.

These pleasant sensations can build up to a much stronger feeling of desire for orgasm, with a full, prickling feeling around the clitoris, but the build-up usually takes a good deal longer for women than it does for men. So the situation often arises that a boy is much more excited by petting, much earlier than a girl is. He will get an erection and an increasing desire to fuck. If he doesn't actually reach a climax during petting (sometimes this is all it takes for a young man) he may begin to feel uncomfortable prickling and congestion in his balls.

When one has reached this stage, such situations can obviously end in intercourse even if many of the requirements for successful love-making are not fulfilled. If it is the first time for one or both partners it may be a great disappointment, however much in love they are. And if one hasn't used any form of contraception the following months may be a nightmare. Indeed, only about one half of young people use contraceptives when they first have intercourse, not having foreseen that their embraces would lead so far.

The notion of responsibility has been abused by an amazing number of parents and writers on sex instruction. But the expression is still a valid one, for there is no denying the fact that some feeling of responsibility for one's fellow beings is tied to a mature emotional life. And these feelings of responsibility are strongest towards those people one cares for most. One may feel justifiably disillusioned when one looks at the world and sees the lack of responsibility and respect for others' life and liberty, especially in political spheres. But you need not despair because the world is in a mess. Feelings of responsibility are to be taken seriously, and falling in love provides one of the first emotional situations in which responsibility for others can prove itself.

For both boys and girls this means taking into account the fact that your partner may have different sexual needs from you. It is particularly important that boys should not expect girls to share their sense of urgency about intercourse; and it can be a positively unpleasant experience if entered into reluctantly. A girl should not be forced into a sexual relationship that she is not happy about; nor should she be expected to accept intercourse as a total substitute for petting once she has experienced it. For most girls intercourse is a component of sex, not the beginning and end of it.

Young people should realize that their desire to be cuddled and caressed will arouse very strong desires in their partners. This build-up of excitement can of course be released through masturbating, both for boys and girls, but it is important not to raise your partner's expectations and then leave him or her 'up in the air'. If you do not want to have intercourse or help him or her to 'come' it is fairer to extricate yourself at an earlier stage if possible. It is not always understood that once a girl has been fully aroused, her need for orgasm is as acute as her partner's, so if you can help each other to have an orgasm it is much pleasanter than slipping off to the bathroom to do it yourself.

In the end, however, it should be kept in mind that the discomfort of intense sexual arousal is not dangerous to the person aroused, and it should not be used as an excuse to force another person to do something they would rather not do. Nobody has this right over another person, and this, the most important aspect of responsibility, applies in non-sexual circumstances as well.

Love and partnership

Young people who have been in love several times, only to see their feelings fade, often wonder how people can manage to live their whole lives together. And of course some can't – so they separate, which is reasonable enough. Some of the couples who carry on living together may not actually care for one another very much but stick together because it's the done thing or for practical reasons, possibly out of consideration for the children. There may also be other, even stranger reasons why two people continue a discordant marriage rather than live alone. If one's own parents are divorced or one suffers from having to listen to their continual squabbles, one may well begin to doubt whether love between two people can really exist.

On the other hand there are those, especially young girls, who place too much faith in the descriptions of love to be found in magazines and other forms of entertainment. Apparently, according to these romanticized accounts, one only has to marry him in order to live happily ever after.

One may imagine that one is experiencing love when one is infatuated. And this is not entirely wide of the mark, since one may feel some of the basic aspects of love: warmth, optimism, interdependence, passion. And some infatuations last and mature into love.

This kind of development demands a great deal of emotional maturity, perseverance and a will to contribute; so unless one can grow out of egoistic feelings, intolerance, and vulnerability, love has little chance of developing. It takes time to build a fruitful and loving relationship and though being in love can help to make it successful this is not essential. There must be continual interaction between the partners, a willingness to learn each other's qualities, peculiarities, and even defects, and to accept them, while continuing to smooth away the rough edges in oneself.

Of course there are people who, while building up loving and sustaining relationships, prefer to do so from the independence of separate homes. But most people, whether they formalize the arrangement or not, decide to live with their partners, both because they want to spend as much time together as possible and for sheer economic reasons. It takes hard work and tolerance to live together, and it takes more than that if you decide to extend your relationship to include children. At every step of the way there may be difficulties, some of them so great that they assume the qualities of a crisis. Some people may give up at this point and extricate themselves. But overcoming such difficulties contributes to the slow growth of maturity, both for each partner separately and together. A relationship in which the partners have been able to develop tolerance, loyalty, co-operation and equality never becomes boring, as some people think. Indeed one's interest in the other person is made more acute because a person who has these qualities will always continue to look outwards.

Sex is important when you really love someone. It should be a permanent ingredient of love and companionship and a means of reconciliation in those crises which even genuinely warm love relationships almost unavoidably run into.

On jealousy

Jealousy can be described as a desperate feeling somewhere between fury and helplessness. As children we may feel jealous of brothers or sisters, thinking that our parents prefer them. As we've mentioned, parents can also feel jealousy towards a boyfriend or girl-friend who they feel is taking their child away from them. But the most painful form of jealousy usually involves someone with whom you are in love. If you fear that they prefer someone else the worry can be torture. You may even have fantasies about hurting them or eliminating your rival. Perhaps you'll imagine fateful car crashes in which the one you love returns to you for comfort.

The trouble with jealousy is that it can gnaw holes in a relationship. This is particularly so when the jealousy is based on suspicion rather than fact. If the person you love feels that he or she is being watched, and isn't trusted, affection can soon turn to irritation; jealousy very often leads to the loss that it wants to prevent.

Probably the worst way of handling jealousy is to keep it to yourself. Try to find someone you can talk to. If your fears are groundless, the simple act of sharing them may make them shrink in front of your eyes. If your lover really is moving away from you, the perfectly understandable pain will be lessened if it is shared.

Jealousy is often connected with insecurity, but it also reflects the idea that feelings and ownership go together. Everyone talks about '*my* husband', '*my* wife', '*my* lover' and so on. We tend to want to own each other, so that if the person you love is 'stolen' from you you feel angry. The idea that loving means owning creates a lot of pain.

Communal living

Communal living is not a new thing. Historically, human beings have always lived together in fairly large family units. It is the tiny 'nuclear' family of two adults and two or three children which is new. And this tiny unit, created at the time of the industrial revolution when families were split up, forced off the land and into factories, has not proved totally satisfactory to everyone. Women with small children suffer particularly from isolation and depression, cut off for hours on end with no adult company.

There is now a small but not insignificant move back into communal living by people who have come to realize that by sharing among a group of people the tasks which have been traditionally seen as 'women's work' – childcare, housework, etc. – they can take a small step towards achieving equality between the sexes. And as an added bonus, they can improve their standard of living by sharing such expensive items as washing machines, cars and so on. 'Communal living' does not necessarily refer only to groups of twenty people in big country houses; it can also cover small groups sharing houses or flats in a city or the more formal arrangement of houses divided into units with some communal space.

Some, though by no means all, people who live communally are also calling into question the whole idea of 'pair bonding'. They feel that exclusive sexual relationships are not necessarily a good thing for society any more than exclusive living arrangements are. This does not mean, however, that communal living provides an opportunity for irresponsible sexual relationships. On the contrary, resentment and jealousy cannot be done away with just by good intentions, so these attempts to broaden human relations and extend the idea of friendship to include sex, require care, tact, compassion and time.

About the following chapters

The next five chapters describe the various elements which help create a successful relationship between two people on a purely sexual level.

As we have said, it is quite possible to have sex and enjoy it without having great affection for one another. But infatuation and love are the strongest foundations on which to build a sexual relationship.

Sex can be the most pleasurable instrument of the feelings, and the sex organs are naturally the most essential tools of sex. We have already seen what the sex organs look like and how they function, but we need to know a great deal more about what they can do in order to enjoy each other fully. Although the art of love has been part of the education of young people in some cultures, it has hitherto been regarded in western society as too risky to describe such techniques to young people as part of sex instruction. This was because of fear based on superstition that they might stimulate curiosity and excite sexual desires to such an extent that the uncritical would hop straight into bed with each other.

During puberty, when by far the majority have not yet tried to have sex, one may often entertain total misconceptions about sexual matters. This leads to one's first experience taking place in an atmosphere of such insecurity and anxiety that it may easily be disappointing, just as a boy may be so nervous that he does not put on a condom even though he has one in his pocket.

In fact the purely technical aspects are simple; anyone can learn how to make love with a little practice. If many people do find difficulties, this is not only due to lack of knowledge but more to mistaken ideas about modesty and lack of trust between the partners. If one doesn't dare express one's sexual desires to one's partner, sex may soon become a miserable business. But in such cases, there may also be something wrong with the emotional aspects of the relationship since love and affection ought to overcome the kind of secrecy which destroys sexual pleasure.

The senses

Humans seem to be made to make love. They have feelings, imagination, memory, as well as lips, tongues and hands; they have eyes, ears, a nose and sex organs, and they have warm rooms in winter. And, unlike other animals, humans have a sexual instinct which functions all year round, with small variations.

Sight

The appearance of the other person is an important erotic stimulus. Not special clothes, because fashions change as the wind blows, but their 'vibrations', their way of moving, their colouring and body. Although society has a particular view of beauty (which changes according to culture and fashion), the old saying that 'love is blind' has a certain truth. Once a relationship is established which goes beyond the superficial first impression, lovers automatically select in each other the things which are unique and special, so that comparison with the ideal becomes irrelevant.

In a sexual situation, the sight of a naked body and the expression of pleasure on a lover's face can add considerably to each person's awareness of the other and their feelings of affection and excitement. So, although some people feel modestly impelled to turn out the light, they may be missing an important dimension of sexuality.

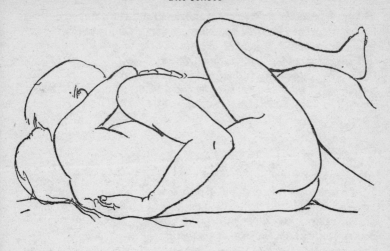

Smell

For many animals, dogs for example, smell is an all-determining factor in the reproduction of the species. When on heat the bitch gives out a strong-smelling secretion from the genitals which can attract the male dog from a considerable distance. The human sense of smell is not nearly as well developed as that of dogs, though our body smell is just as strong. Even so our appreciation of each other is incredibly affected by smell. Without noticing it and without even knowing it we divide the people around us into those who have a strongly scented smell, those with a more neutral smell and those who smell nasty.

Bad breath can really be unpleasant – a fact which toothpaste advertisements outrival each other in exaggerating. Just changing the kind of toothpaste you use is not the important thing; the reasons are more complicated than that (see p. 127).

Clean sweat can smell good and may be an erotic stimulant, but stale sweat gives off a rancid smell. Daily washing will keep your skin clean enough, but if you do not find that sufficiently effective, you will find further advice on p. 128.

As we have described earlier, the membranes of our sex organs secrete a waxy secretion of which the smell is an erotic stimulus and grows stronger as we get sexually aroused. The obsession of our hygienic era with dirt and the intimate connection between the sex organs and the excreta of the urethra and the anus have resulted in widespread aversion to sexual smells also.

The sex organs must be washed, preferably daily, but some people may find extra pleasure in not washing immediately before intercourse – they like themselves and others to smell human.

Hearing

We can also receive erotic stimuli through the ear. Some people enjoy love-making to the accompaniment of music – the movements of intercourse are directed by the rhythms. Other people find mechanically produced sounds distracting.

The amorous voice of the partner can be exciting in itself, though some people also like hearing 'dirty' words – or saying them.

As intercourse progresses many lovers become increasingly disposed to utter groaning or whimpering noises. These are a wordless confirmation of pleasure and thus have a stimulatory effect on the other person.

Quite often the vagina makes 'farting' noises during intercourse, especially if the penis is drawn right out with each backward pull. This is because all air is expelled from the vagina when the penis is pushed back in so that as the penis is withdrawn the air is sucked back into the vagina and sets the lubricated membranes vibrating as it passes along the walls. This sound is quite natural and nothing to be embarrassed about, just as there is no need to worry if the vagina makes slurping noises, which are merely indications that it is well moist. But you can always try another position; this will often make any noises disappear.

Touch

Certain areas of the body are more sensitive than others. Many people, though not everybody, are excited by being tickled or stroked in the nape of the neck, for example, in the ears, on the lips, on the palms of the hands, around the navel and along the vertebrae. Women's nipples are very sensitive to the touch and stand erect when caressed, and often a man may be just as excited by fondling a woman's breasts as she is by his doing so.

The most powerful sensations are produced by touching the sex organs and the area around them. The most sensitive part of the woman is the clitoris and of the man the head of the penis.

The excitement of feeling another person's body against one's own is usually an ingredient of every sexual situation. Indeed, it has such a thrilling effect on some people that even when they are separated from their partner's body by clothes they can reach a climax just by dancing together and pressing themselves against each other.

Kissing

The members of some primitive societies never kiss — they rub noses instead. For us a kiss is felt to be essential as a form of expression, though some individual people shrink from 'love kisses'.

But a kiss is many different things. It may be the dry kiss we give to parents, aunts and so on, or a form of greeting between friends. An erotic kiss is something completely different. The first one may be fumbling and unsure, an attempt to imitate what you have seen in old films — a dry, protracted, lip-to-lip kiss. Gradually you learn to part your lips and let your tongue play with the tongue and teeth of the other person. It can be a beautiful, exciting experience and stimulates the production of saliva so that you feel as if you are 'drinking from each other'.

In an erotic situation you will also want to kiss and be kissed on other parts of the body, and those places we have described as being the most sensitive to the touch will obviously be equally susceptible to kisses, licking and sucking. There are also many people who like nibbling each other, though this requires a certain amount of caution, especially around the sex organs.

Making love without intercourse

Making love is an experience which includes all the ways in which people have learned to please each other physically since their earliest sexual experiences. There is no sense in which young people 'graduate' from the kissing and cuddling of their first relationships to a new 'adult' form of sex. Rather, they should learn new ways of pleasing each other and add them on. Intercourse (fucking) is part of love-making but not all of it, and it is perfectly possible to enjoy sex and find it satisfying without having intercourse at all. If you do decide to include fucking in your love-making, it is very important to avoid an *unwanted pregnancy*, so do get some advice about contraception first (see pp. 86–106).

In this chapter we are going to look first at ways of making love without intercourse. For many men and women this way of making love together may be extremely satisfying though there are some people for whom love-making isn't complete without intercourse. Nevertheless, the avoidance of intercourse is the best way of avoiding pregnancy, so, if you don't have contraceptives, or you are unsure of their safety, and you are certain you don't want to have a baby, it makes sense to learn how best to satisfy each other safely.

One of the great advantages of making love like this is that you learn to recognize each other's responses more quickly because you have to pay more attention to your partner. In fact it is often much easier for a woman to have an orgasm this way than through intercourse, because her lover can concentrate on the more sensitive parts of her body directly. For their part, men can begin to learn about sensations of their own that they have never experienced before, because the more exploratory nature of this way of making love gives men the opportunity to discover that, like women, their bodies are enormously sensitive to caresses all over.

But successful love-making doesn't happen in real life like it does in the movies with bells ringing and music playing! It requires both initiative and independence. Both partners must learn to talk intimately with one another and have the courage to show each other what feels best.

Orgasm without intercourse

Making love is not always something you have decided to do. It may develop gradually. You kiss and caress each other, eventually find your way under each other's clothes, become less inhibited and more bold, more or less undress each other and begin to search with your hands for the other person's sex organs.

One day one of you has an orgasm and for a while you may continue just to achieve this again, but gradually – or so one hopes – a mutual wish develops for the other person to achieve a climax too.

The woman

Lack of experience in the woman, and ignorance about her sexual responses on the part of the man, may mean that the man has greater difficulty satisfying a girl than the other way round. If she has never masturbated to orgasm she cannot tell him exactly what he should do. The man should continue to experiment, with guidance from the woman. Sometimes, however, the problem may prove insoluble, in which case it may help if she learns to masturbate and conveys her experiences to him.

As we have said, the clitoris is the most sensitive part of the woman. The exact position of it can be seen in the illustration on p. 27. Her partner can try rubbing it gently, making sure that it is well moistened. If not, he can take some of the lubricating fluid from the vagina or possibly use spit.

If she likes what he is doing and can't suggest anything better, then he is on the right track. As he carries on she will gradually become more and more excited. Then something unexpected may happen: it feels as if part of the clitoris is disappearing under your finger. The man may take this incorrectly as a sign that she has come and if she does not know what an orgasm is she may even resign herself to the removal of his finger without complaining. In this way, the whole business may prove one-sided and unsatisfactory for her because her body has become excited and she is not able to find any release.

What happens is that when a woman reaches a certain degree of sexual excitement, the clitoris is drawn back and up under a fold of skin. It is a sign that she is well on the way, but not there yet. If the man allows his finger to slide up in the same direction as the clitoris he will be able to feel it under the fold of skin and continue in the same way he began. If he cannot find it properly, then she should help him. If she is still satisfied with the way he is rubbing her, then it should not be long before she reaches orgasm.

At the approach of and immediately after orgasm the clitoris may become extremely sensitive and the woman may find it virtually insupportable to be touched there. This does not necessarily mean that she has come as much as she wants to. As we have said, some women can have several orgasms one after another, and it would be a shame for her not to have the rest. So after stopping for a little while, the man can try gently rubbing her again if she still wants him to. It should be remembered, however, that not all women want, or can achieve, a succession of orgasms; and one orgasm if it is satisfying is no better or worse than several.

Some women cannot stand direct contact on the clitoris – they find it downright painful. If this is the case, the man can try putting a couple of fingers around the clitoris and moving them rhythmically, for example, or pushing the mons veneris (the mound with hair on) backwards and forwards a bit with his fingers or the flat of his hand. There are also several other possibilities, and since the man cannot guess beforehand what is going to be best for the woman, *she* should control the direction, pressure and speed of what he does. It sounds very simple but can be really difficult before you 'hit on the right tune', so to speak.

One of the reasons why we have discussed satisfying the woman first is because it is most gratifying for both partners if she reaches orgasm before he does (unless, of course, you are aiming at simultaneous orgasm, in which case see below). For after the man has reached orgasm, and he tends to come more quickly, he may sometimes lose his sexual appetite to such an extent that he is no longer interested in satisfying the woman. He may not even have the energy. But the woman's sexual excitement diminishes more slowly, and even after orgasm she usually still has the energy to carry on and help him to a climax.

The man

There are a number of ways in which a girl can satisfy a boy. If it is the first time, a girl may feel too shy to do so actively. This can create problems if the boy is shy as well and doesn't feel able to ask her to help. It is possible for him to reach a climax with his penis between her thighs, but this is a bit risky because, if he is lying too far up, some of the semen may find its way into the vagina and result in pregnancy (yes, it has happened!). Usually the man will ask her to hold his penis in her hands while he makes the movements to achieve climax. Of course she can make the movements herself, bringing her hands up and down over the penis, but in this case it is important that *he* should show *her* the correct way to do it and that she should ask him. Alternatively, either of them can hold her breasts together making a kind of 'sheath' around his penis while he sits astride her, or she can hold his penis under her arm. Some kind of lubricant makes these methods feel better.

Variations

You can start by licking each other's sex organs until you reach orgasm. For this, the man should kneel forwards between the spread legs of the woman and find the clitoris with his tongue. He then makes the same movements with his tongue as he would with his fingers until she reaches orgasm. Every now and again he can vary this by licking her on the labia and a little way up into the vagina, but the main pressure should fall on or around the clitoris. He may

61

also give her even greater pleasure by putting a finger up into the vagina while he is licking her (there is generally room to do this even if she is still a virgin), and then, when she comes, he will be able to notice how the walls of the vagina contract rhythmically around his finger.

She can satisfy him by kneeling forwards between his legs in the same way and taking the head of the penis in her mouth. She can support the penis in her hand, pull the foreskin (if he has one) right back and then begin moving her lips up and down over the top. At the same time, she can suck and rub with her tongue.

Many girls will pull their heads away when the semen comes. This is usually unsatisfying for him unless she finishes him off with her hand. Quite a few men have a more or less hidden desire for their partner to take the semen in their mouths. Many women have a deeply rooted objection to this, whereas others are quite content with it. Admittedly it seldom has a sexually exciting effect on the woman.

The woman must be careful not to bite the penis, since her teeth can easily tear holes in the membrane. Instead she can suck the underneath of the head of the penis and rub it with her tongue until he has an orgasm, since this is the most sensitive area.

If you want to reach orgasm at the same time, or almost the same time, you can try lying in such a way that the man has his head in the woman's crotch and she has his penis in her mouth. This position is called sixty-nine because the two numbers, when put side by side, look like two people making love in this way. If you can work out how to do it, it can be very satisfying, though when the man is much taller than the woman, or the other way round, you may find it difficult for both of you to reach each other's sex organs at the same time.

You must remember that the woman should *never* lie underneath the man, as she may be choked by the semen (this has been known to happen).

The possibilities we have discussed here should give you a pretty good indication of how you can have a pleasant, varied and exciting sexual relationship even though actual intercourse is 'not on'. This is not to say that all the possibilities have been exhausted, and it must be stressed that no variations, however peculiar, which are used by a loving couple to excite and satisfy each other can be called 'perverted' (i.e. sexually sick or abnormal) as long as they are agreed about what they are doing and not worried by anything. Take anal eroticism, for example. It is not unusual for one or both of you to put a finger into the anus in certain sexual positions, e.g. sixty-nine. Many people find it surprisingly pleasurable.

It is less common for a man and a woman to have anal intercourse, although this is one of the ways in which homosexual men make love. If you do try it, take it gently. The muscles of the anus are not as flexible as the vagina and can easily be painfully strained. It is also possible to cause haemorrhoids (varicose veins at the opening of the anus) or tear the membrane. To avoid damage, it is important to use plenty of lubrication on the penis (vaseline or KY Jelly).

For heterosexual couples, one of the dangers is the possibility of transferring bacteria from the anus to the vagina. Bacteria which cause no problem in the anus can cause infection once transferred to the moist environment of the vagina. So avoid putting a finger, penis, or anything else which has been in the anus, into the vagina without washing it first.

Where does intercourse come in?

As we said at the beginning, there are many advantages to making love without intercourse. Not only do you have no worries about contraception, but you also have an opportunity to get to know your own and your partner's responses much better. But for most young people there will come a time when you start to have vague feelings of dissatisfaction. It may be simple curiosity to know what intercourse feels like, or it may be a sense of incompleteness, a desire to take your loving further. In this case, you would be well advised to start using contraception (see pp. 86–106) and include intercourse in your love-making.

Intercourse

There are dozens of common expressions for intercourse. 'Coitus' is the technical term but you are more likely to hear 'make love', 'fuck', 'go to bed together' or 'screw'. They all of course describe the sexual activity when a man's erect penis is put into a woman's vagina. Intercourse is usually preceded by a period of foreplay.

Foreplay

By 'foreplay' we mean loveplay which takes place before intercourse. Foreplay is perhaps the wrong word for it because it actually includes all the kissing and caressing of making love of which intercourse is only a part. For most people, and girls in particular, the whole atmosphere in which love-making occurs is an important part of it. Most girls are more easily distracted and may not be able to concentrate on the sensations which excite them if they are afraid of interruptions or feel insecure about the place, the person, or the possibility of pregnancy.

During foreplay, we use our bodies, our tongues, fingers, senses and imagination (in fact everything we have described in the last two chapters) to excite ourselves and our partner in readiness for intercourse. Some people take longer than others to become aroused, and women nearly always take longer than men. An erection is the obvious sign of arousal for men; with women it is less obvious but just as important; the vaginal wall secretes a lubricant which makes fucking pleasant for both partners. If the vagina is not wet the friction from the penis rubbing against it can be most unpleasant.

Intercourse for the first time

Many young women are afraid of fucking because they have read or been told that it is very painful the first time. Certainly most girls have a hymen (see p. 26) partially blocking the vagina, and it is the breaking of this hymen which can hurt and bleed a little. However, the discomfort will be minimized if you or your partner gently but firmly press the hymen back against the sides of your vagina each day for a couple of weeks or so before attempting intercourse. A man should never attempt penetration before his partner is completely aroused, and this is particularly important the first time, because the natural lubrication of the vagina will make penetration a great deal easier for both of you. If it does hurt you should stop, and try again another day. Each time you will be stretching the hymen a little more. If penetration seems impossible, you may be one of the very few women who have a hymen so thick that it should be removed surgically by a doctor.

If, even with gentleness and patience, you are unable to have intercourse it could be that the problem is a little more complicated. We discuss problems on pp. 76–8.

Intercourse

When both partners are fully aroused one or other of them can guide the erect penis into the vagina. It is usually better if the woman does this, parting the lips of her labia at the same time. This ensures that the penis gets to the right place and that no hairs or folds of the labia get caught (ouch)! One or both partners then move their pelvis and possibly their whole body so that the penis slides backwards and forwards in the vagina. After a certain amount of time, which may vary from a few minutes to an hour or so, these movements create an increasing sensation of pleasure which may spread up from the sex organs to the whole body. Then, and for most women this requires a certain amount of stimulation with the fingers as well as the penis, the muscles become tense, respiration more violent, and the movements often grow quicker and deeper until intercourse culminates in one or both partners reaching a climax (i.e. orgasm).

Many women do not have orgasms during intercourse even with extra stimulation with the fingers. In this case, one or other partner can bring her to orgasm afterwards through masturbation. It is quite common for young women to have difficulty coming at all; this is discussed further on pp. 78–80.

Positions

Intercourse can be accomplished in many different positions. The most common is that in which the woman lies on her back with her legs apart and slightly bent at the hips and knees, while the man lies above her with his legs together, supporting himself on his knees and elbows so as not to be too heavy. This position can be varied. The woman, for example, can try bending her hips further towards her, possibly by putting her legs up over the man's shoul-

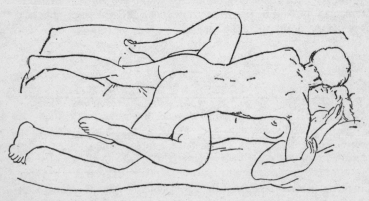

Intercourse.

ders while he gets up on to his hands. It can sometimes help, especially if you are lying on something soft, to support her bottom with pillows or cushions so that the clitoris is in a more impressionable position.

Alternatively the man can lie down and the woman can sit astride him with one leg on either side. In this position the woman has more control over the speed and depth of movements. She can also position herself in such a way that the movements of the penis give maximum stimulation to the clitoris, and she can easily increase the stimulation by rubbing with her own fingers.

The position where the man lies behind the woman also provides greater possibilities for manual stimulation by either partner which increases the chances of orgasm for the woman. In this position the woman lies on her side and the man enters from behind. It is unlikely that a woman would reach orgasm in this position without manual stimulation because the penis does not rub against the area which encloses the clitoris.

These two 'variations' may be the most satisfactory for women who cannot reach orgasm by intercourse alone but who enjoy the sensation of orgasm during intercourse rather than just by manual stimulation.

In addition of course there are dozens of other positions, sitting, standing or lying down. Anything is acceptable as long as it's possible, but make sure that your partner is equally enthusiastic before you indulge in athletics. Some people find exotic variations distinctly unerotic, particularly if they tend to be 'turned on' by closeness and gentleness. If on the other hand you find variations exciting but can only come in one position there is nothing to stop you changing positions several times, coming back to the one you feel confident with to finish off. Young men should perhaps be wary of wild variations, however, if they have not yet learned how to control orgasm. No woman is going to be happy about trying positions which excite their partners so much that the whole thing is over in two seconds.

Afterwards

There is a wonderful feeling of peace, relaxation and closeness which follows warm and satisfying love-making. For many people this feeling blends into almost immediate sleep. But, particularly at the start of a relationship, it can also be a time when people who love each other feel most open and honest and are able to talk about their deepest feelings. Moments like these often form the strongest bonds in a relationship.

If, however, sex has not been the product of a caring relationship the moments after intercourse can be a real let-down. It can feel very lonely if after sharing such intimacy with a person you then see them turn over and go to sleep (or get up and dress) without a tender word or gentle caress.

Can one make love during a period?

Attitudes vary enormously on this. There is certainly no reason why you shouldn't, but some people simply find it distasteful. Some women feel quite unwell at the start of a period and aren't at all interested in sex. Others may be happy to fuck during a period at the start of a relationship but, once the initial excitement has worn off, they may prefer to wait a few days rather than get blood stains on the sheets!

One simple way of dealing with a messy blood flow is to use a diaphragm (cap). This will hold back the blood flow for a few hours. A diaphragm should be removed and washed out with the same frequency as you would change a tampon.

As there are some women and men who are put off by the thought or presence of blood during love-making, neither partner should insist on doing so. On the other hand, there really isn't anything dirty or nasty about menstrual bleeding, and learning to accept that particular bodily function is a step on the way to feeling comfortable with the totality of your body and your sexual and reproductive functions.

Sexual response and orgasm

As we have now stated several times, certain influences on the sexual organs result in an increased state of sexual tension which can be relieved after a certain period of time in orgasm. So it is time to describe what actually happens and what a man and a woman feel.

Orgasm is also called satisfaction, sexual release, sexual climax or just climax, and to have an orgasm can be called to 'come', to 'give', to 'shoot', to be 'satisfied' or 'gratified' and to 'achieve a climax' – we have already used several of these expressions.

Sexual excitement in women

As women become sexually aroused a number of physiological changes take place in their breasts, sex organs and skin.

The nipples become erect, the breasts swell, and, as excitement increases, the brown area around the nipples swells up so that it can sometimes look as if the nipples have suddenly lost their firmness.

Excitement in the genitals causes the vagina to produce lubricating fluid which then leaks down to moisten the entrance. The clitoris and the labia minora swell and change colour and the labia majora open outwards to make room for the penis to enter. In addition a flush very often spreads over the front of the body.

As sexual tension rises, the clitoris is drawn back and up under

69

the fold of the skin. The inner two thirds of the vagina expand, while the outer third swells. If the woman is having intercourse at this stage the man may be able to feel these changes in the vagina as a firm tightening around his penis.

Orgasm in women

Orgasm entails a series of brief, rhythmical contractions or 'spasms' in that part of the vagina which has swollen up. In addition there will be similar contractions in the womb and possibly in the floor of the pelvis and the anal sphincter.

After orgasm, the changed areas of the body revert to normal quite quickly, though at different rates. Thus the swollen brown area around the nipples will decrease again more quickly than the actual nipples, so they may suddenly look as though they are beginning to stand erect again.

During masturbation (either being petted or on one's own) consciousness of pleasure is concentrated in the clitoris. The constant, uniformly rhythmical rubbing provokes increasingly intense sensations of enjoyment in and around the clitoris and these gradually spread up into the vagina. Eventually these sensations are mingled with a powerful feeling of warmth which travels from the pelvis over the whole body. When the outer third of the vagina swells it will feel as if a contraction were taking place there. Sensual pleasure will have now reached its highest peak and will be concentrated into a pulsating, throbbing sensation in the clitoris and the vagina, corresponding to the stage at which the outer part of the vagina is rhythmically contracted. This pulsating feeling may spread to the whole of the body and finally seem as though it has synchronized with the heartbeat. At the height of orgasm many women also feel an enjoyable tingling in their tensed muscles and even have the sensation that their brain has become temporarily disconnected.

As we have mentioned earlier, in many women one orgasm can succeed another without any drop in the level of excitement between the two. After a single orgasm, however, or a series of several, an agreeable relaxation and general decrease in tension will run through the body and muscles and a drowsy peace will fall over the woman.

For women experiencing orgasm during intercourse the sensation will, broadly speaking, take the same course, except that it is seldom as intense as during masturbation (though it may be more emotionally satisfying). This is because the clitoris is not exposed to such direct pressure during intercourse as it is during other forms of release.

Other women experience orgasm during intercourse as an apparently deeper sensation, and they may have a strong desire to feel the penis right up in the end of the vagina. In fact, reaching a climax may depend on this, in spite of the fact that there are few actual nerve endings in the wall of the vagina itself. The chief reason for the release of sexual tension in orgasm during intercourse is the indirect stimulation of the clitoris, produced by the compression together of the pubic bones and the pushing on the labia as the penis is drawn between them.

So all orgasms actually originate in the clitoris, and an orgasm which is experienced in the vagina is no better or worse than one which is experienced locally in the clitoris.

All that we have said so far has been about physical responses and sensations. In sex this is never the whole story, and even the least involved man or woman will have emotional involvement at some level with every partner. Even masturbation almost always involves certain fantasies. When a young man masturbates, however 'clinically' he may start – perhaps merely to relieve his tension or frustration, which may have been completely non-sexual in origin – as masturbation develops towards orgasm, he will generally develop fantasies of some kind or another. A similar thing may occur whenever a girl masturbates.

There is nothing standardized or uniform about the emotions men and women experience during sex. A relationship of tenderness, love, sharing and giving, with a multitude of other positive emotional qualities on either side, is achieved remarkably frequently, but sex between two people who do not even like one another cannot in itself create this relationship. It is not unusual for many other powerful emotions to be released by sex, such as jealousy or the desire for revenge, domination and to hurt or to be hurt. Many young men and women have been deeply frightened to experience such strong and unpleasant feelings released within themselves by sex; occasionally the experience can be so traumatic that a period of revulsion, sometimes with actual aversion or impotence, can result. Sadly, most men and women find it very difficult to talk about such things, even to their lovers – or, perhaps, particularly to their lovers – and suffer much guilt in the belief that they are abnormally disturbed by sex.

Sexual excitement in men

When the man is sexually stimulated, the spongy tissue of the penis is filled with blood which is pumped in through a 'sluice' so that it cannot flow back. This means that the penis becomes stiff, firm and much larger, until finally it stands erect away from the body, tilted slightly upwards and possibly very slightly to one side. This is called an erection or a 'hard-on'. When the man is extremely excited a couple of drops of clear lubricating fluid may also run out of the urethra.

Gradually, as sexual tension progesses, the balls will also swell and both the scrotum and the balls will be drawn up towards the floor of the pelvis, where they will remain during climax. If the man is sexually aroused for some time *without* having an orgasm, he may experience some pain in the balls because they have become so large and strained.

Just as in women, a flush may appear over the front of the body of an excited man.

Some young women feel a little frightened when they see a naked man with an erection for the first time. It may be difficult to imagine how there could be room for it inside her; but, as we have already pointed out, the vagina is very elastic, and there isn't anything to worry about.

Orgasm in men

During orgasm a number of muscular contractions take place which finally result in the prepared semen being squirted out through the opening of the urethra (the 'eye' in the head of the penis). These contractions rhythmically divide the semen into small portions. This stage corresponds to the point in a woman's orgasm when the swollen walls of the vagina are rhythmically drawn together. The man's anal sphincter may also move.

In contrast to many women, by far the majority of men can achieve only one orgasm at a time; that is to say, it will normally take at least half an hour and maybe several hours before a man can get another erection and reach a new climax. The number of times a young man can reach orgasm during the space of six hours, for example, varies a great deal with the individual. It may be anything between one and five to six times. So as long as you can manage it once there is no need to worry.

Just like women, men can experience the physiological aspects of orgasm in different ways, but for them the difference lies more in the strength and intensity of the sensation than in its point of departure. The greater the amount of semen the longer and more powerful the climax will be, another reason why the first orgasm in a night, for example, is usually the best.

Both during masturbation and intercourse, the regular pressure on the penis will result in increasing physical pleasure, a feeling which is most strongly concentrated in the head of the penis, but also spreads into the floor of the pelvis and, in some people, up over the whole body. The man also sometimes experiences a feeling of warmth.

Just before climax he will notice that the semen is on its way and at a certain point he will find it impossible to control his responses. The semen is going to be released whether he wants it or not. The height of orgasm is reached immediately before and during the first muscular contractions which push forward the semen. And, just as in women, orgasm may be accompanied by a luxurious tension in the muscles and followed by relaxation and a dozy feeling of comfort.

A few more words about orgasm

Although both male and female orgasm presupposes some physical stimulation of the sex organs in by far the majority of cases, the following examples will show that this kind of influence is not always necessary.

When asleep, both sexes may have such erotic dreams that they reach orgasm – you may find yourself waking up in the middle of climax. If you have a great many erotic dreams, they may be interpreted as a sign that you do not get the necessary degree of satisfaction for your sexual needs when you are awake.

It is also possible for certain men and women to reach a sexual climax solely by listening to particularly stimulating music, reading suggestive or exciting books or seeing similar pictures or films. Moreover, some women may reach orgasm solely by stimulation of the nipples. Perhaps the strangest thing is that men can ejaculate involuntarily if they are suddenly overcome by powerful feelings of worry or panic (during some kind of disaster, for example).

All these things just go to show how complicated the orgasmic reaction really is.

Older people

Those sexual reactions which are purely physiological tend to decrease in sensitivity and intensity to a certain extent with age, although women often find their sex peak at around thirty, when experience and self-confidence have increased their ability to enjoy sex. Changes in sexual needs and capabilities vary greatly with the individual and are especially susceptible to mental factors.

To generalize, one can say that the more one cultivates the sexual side of life, the better one will preserve sexual vitality through the years. This applies to both men and women.

Some young people are unhappy at the thought that their parents and even grandparents still have an active sex life. In my opinion, one should be glad that such a rich source of sexual and emotional experience can be drawn on throughout one's life.

Group sex

Relationships in which more than two people participate and have sexual intercourse together usually happen in threes or fours, e.g. two women and one man, two men and one women, or two men and two women. They can have intercourse at the same time or alternately. This may happen spontaneously, or it may be a planned sexual experiment where feelings are not very much involved. However, it is not really within the scope of this book to elaborate further.

Difficulties
with sex

However natural sex may be, the enjoyment of it doesn't always come easily. Sadly, many people are not enjoying it at all, or certainly not as much as they could do. The reasons for such problems can be very simple or they can be more complex. Often they are rooted in feelings of guilt and embarrassment which we've picked up unconsciously from family or friends. Probably the first golden rule in dealing with difficulties is to *talk* about it – preferably with your partner but also with other friends you feel you can trust. You may find that your difficulty is a common one that others have learned to deal with or have simply grown out of. Just that knowledge can be such a relief that the problem stops being a problem.

When intercourse seems impossible

Most women are at least a little bit afraid the first time they have intercourse. They may be afraid that it will hurt (see p. 65 on how this can be minimized), or they may be afraid of pregnancy or quite simply of sex itself. This fear can cause the muscles around the vagina to contract so that penetration is quite painful, if not impossible. For most women, time and consideration are all that will be necessary for those muscles to relax, but a few women have such a deep-seated fear of penetration that their muscles clench up at even the slightest touch. This condition is know as vaginismus.

It is absolutely no help whatever for a man to force his way in; in fact this will only make matters worse. A vagina which tightens up is doing so in self-defence, and it is important to discover why the woman needs such a defence. The reaction could well be triggered by some past sexual experience, a rape, for example; or it could be based on feelings of guilt about having sex.

While the problem persists, it is wise to avoid attempts at intercourse and to concentrate on petting. The realization that you can enjoy yourselves without intercourse should take some of the tension out of the situation, and in the meantime the woman can try to help herself. It is common for a woman with vaginismus to be unable even to insert a tampon or put one of her own fingers into her vagina. She will need to overcome her own inhibitions before she will feel sufficiently relaxed to allow anyone else that close. The first step is for her to explore her own body in private, gradually accustoming herself to allowing first one, and then two, of her own fingers to explore the inside of her vagina. Once she feels more confident she may be able to allow her partner to do the same thing; but whatever happens, it should be taken slowly.

If this doesn't work, try one of the books or advice centres listed on pp. 135–7 for more guidance.

Pains during intercourse

Most women experience some pain the first time they have intercourse, although this can be minimized (see p. 65). Apart from this, if intercourse is painful there is something wrong. Sometimes a woman can feel a dull ache if the man thrusts too hard and too deeply during intercourse. This is particularly likely in positions in which the vagina is shortened, for example when the woman lies on her back with her knees drawn up or kneels forward with the man behind her. If the woman lies flat her vagina will straighten out and if she sits on top of the man, she can herself control the depth of penetration. As we are all made in different shapes, the most comfortable positions will vary from one couple to another. It is worth noting also that the uterus moves slightly at different stages in the menstrual cycle, so that what hurts one week may feel fine the next.

Vaginal dryness can be another source of discomfort. If you continue fucking without enough lubrication, the vaginal walls will be rubbed raw. This not only hurts at the time; it can take a few days to heal and can additionally make the woman feel very apprehensive about intercourse next time. As nervousness is one of the main reasons for lack of lubrication, this can create a cycle which is difficult to break and sex will seem pretty miserable.

Lack of lubrication is very often due to haste on the part of the man and insufficient confidence on the part of the woman to tell him that he is going too fast. Sometimes, though, all that is needed to stimulate the natural production of lubrication, and at the same time make the woman feel more aroused, is the use of an artificial lubricant. KY Jelly can be bought at any chemist for this purpose; otherwise a spermicidal cream or jelly or even saliva will do (don't use vaseline). But do remember that artificial wetness shouldn't be used to replace natural wetness, merely to stimulate it. If a woman is not producing it herself she may well be unhappy with sex and it would be better to talk about it.

Difficulty with orgasm – women

This is probably one of the commonest sex problems. The simple fact is that many women have to learn how to have orgasms; they don't always flow automatically from having sex, no matter how loving the relationship is. There is a common but unfortunate belief among young people that a woman can only be taught how to enjoy sex by a man. The result is that some women go from one lover to another in search of the man who will be able to 'unlock the secret of her orgasm'. In fact no one is better able to understand a woman's sexual response than she is herself. Certainly a skilful and thoughtful lover is a great help in making the discovery and can be invaluable in ensuring that you enjoy it, but nobody can tell you how to feel; this section will only show you the best ways of discovering how your body works.

The first thing to understand is that you are extremely unlikely to get fully sexually aroused if you are anxious about getting pregnant, afraid of taking too long or simply not interested in sex. Arousal and orgasm are almost as dependent on your state of mind as on your body. It is quite possible to appear aroused and yet be totally unprepared mentally. One of the greatest blocks to really letting yourself go is the tendency to watch your own reactions rather than experiencing them. If you are wondering how you look, or if what you are doing is correct, you are not allowing your mind to receive signals from your body. So try to stop thinking and start feeling.

If you are still having difficulties, you are more likely to learn about your responses from masturbation than from fucking because the sensations are more direct. Many women find it easier to learn to masturbate on their own when they don't have to concern themselves with another person's feelings and reactions. Since learning to enjoy sex is primarily a question of learning how to please yourself, masturbation, in privacy, is a good starting point.

It is not hard to find your own clitoris. Your sensations (and the diagram on p. 27) will direct you to the most sensitive place. Now, start by using some kind of lubricant (this is always very important; if the clitoris is dry it can hurt). Then stroke the whole area before concentrating on the place where it feels best. Your stroking should be regular and sustained; your own sensations will tell you how hard to press and what speed suits you. Don't be surprised if it takes a long time the first time; up to one hour is not unusual. You may find that it is easier at first with the help of a vibrator. These are often described as 'personal massagers' and are available from sex shops, chemists, and by mail order. A massager is quite expensive, but if it works for you you will probably feel it was worth it. They are usually made in an unmistakable 'phallic' shape, though the vibration is more effective on or near the clitoris than in the vagina.

Once you've learned how to have orgasms yourself you can much more easily teach someone else to do it to you. You may also find that it happens quite easily during intercourse, but don't be disappointed if it doesn't. Many women need a little extra stimulation during intercourse and so they use a position which enables them, or their partner, to touch the clitoris at the same time. As we've mentioned before, it often takes longer for a woman to become aroused than for a man, so if a man doesn't have enough control over his own orgasm to ensure that it isn't all over in seconds it is unlikely that she will be able to come. This sort of control can take some time to learn, so in the meantime you should concentrate on petting, making fucking only a small part of your love-making and the man should ensure that his partner is satisfied afterwards through masturbation.

Once you have both learned a little more about your own reactions you might find that particular positions suit you best. Many people find that the position when the man is on top brings the clitoris into closest contact with the man's pubic bone. You may also learn to squeeze your pelvic floor muscles (the ones which control urine flow as well) which brings your clitoris into closer contact with the penis. If you take a long time to get fully aroused, you will probably find that sustained, rhythmic fucking is more satisfying than wild changes of position and tempo.

If you seem to be making very little progress you may want to read one of the books listed at the end or find out about counselling (see pp. 135–7). Whatever you decide, try not to make the attainment of orgasm the focus of your relationship. Enjoy what is best about sex together and concentrate on what you can get out of it. If the attainment of orgasm becomes your major goal you may well find yourself losing what pleasure you already share in sex together.

Premature ejaculation

By premature ejaculation we mean exactly what we say, that the man's orgasm comes and the semen is released long before it is intended. If the young man is intensely excited sexually, ejaculation may occur before he enters the vagina or immediately after he has done so. A pleasure that is over that quickly is clearly not as enjoyable as one that lasts a while, and this is particularly so for his partner, who may only just be getting interested when the man has an orgasm and loses his erection.

Obviously the first time you have intercourse you may be excited and nervous and it can happen very easily. If there are long gaps between sexual encounters then intercourse may again feel so new and exciting that it is impossible for the man to control himself.

It does not matter terribly if the first orgasm comes too early, as most young men will be potent again after half an hour to two hours, and the intervening time can be used for foreplay.

If it only takes a few coital movements to bring you to a second orgasm, then this will create greater problems. If you have the time, and your partner is still interested, you can wait for a third erection, by which time you may be sufficiently desensitized to sustain an erection. Unfortunately few people have the time and privacy necessary to deal with the matter this way, so you may have to try more practical methods. The man can try masturbating beforehand. This will ensure that his sensitivity is slightly decreased. Or he can use a condom, if he isn't doing so already, because this should also decrease sensitivity.

If the problem persists, there is a technique called the 'squeeze' technique, which is described more fully in one of the books mentioned on p. 137 (*Treat Yourself to Sex*). It involves masturbating almost to orgasm and then squeezing the tip of the penis until the urge recedes, and then starting again. It is an effective therapy, but it doesn't work for everyone. If you still cannot manage to keep an erection long enough, you may need some personal counselling. On the other hand, if you are young, and don't have a regular girlfriend, don't worry too much. The problem will probably sort itself out in time. One thing to keep in mind is that nobody can keep an erection long enough for a woman to have an orgasm if the problem is her own lack of knowledge or inhibition. So, if you haven't already done so, read the section on problems with orgasm for women.

Absence of ejaculation

Some boys cannot reach orgasm however hard they try. This may be due to nerves or to the fact that you do not really care very much for your partner. However, you will usually be able to reach orgasm and ejaculation by masturbating. If you can't even do this, then it is probably because you are too young and not sufficiently mature sexually.

Both women and men have difficulty in reaching orgasm after drinking alcohol, since alcohol reduces sensitivity in the sex organs. And some men experience these kinds of difficulties when they use a condom; if so, it would be better if the couple used some other form of contraception.

Impotence

Impotence is an inability to carry intercourse through to orgasm. The condition described as 'absence of ejaculation' is a kind of impotence, though usually the word 'impotence' is used to mean an inability to achieve an erection in those situations where it is called for.

Many young men become more or less impotent the first time they go to bed with a woman. This is due to a strong sense of anticipation and over-excitement. It is as if you are sitting an examination and your mind goes blank, even though you knew the answers perfectly well before you sat down.

But impotence is also a very common occurrence in later sexual relationships, especially when you are going to bed with a woman with whom you are not entirely relaxed. It is likely that the more you care for her the more easily you will find yourself impotent, since her opinion of you matters a great deal. Obviously the less interested you are in somebody the less vulnerable you are to their opinions.

The source of a great deal of impotence lies in the fact that people are more prone to boasting and exaggeration about their sex lives – about the size of their penis, their ability to make love or their potency – than about any other area of experience. If you are credulous and swallow all your friends' stories, you may begin to feel inferior, even if you are a keen boaster yourself. So when you are about to go to bed with a woman, your feelings of inferiority may intrude, especially if you know that she has made love with other people and is in a position to make comparisons.

A young man who has pretended to his friends of both sexes that he is an unbeatable lover and who then finds himself justifiably doubtful about his sexual superiority may well be abandoned by the potency he worships. He will feel wounded and humiliated by the situation, almost irreparably so.

Any kind of impotence can become a vicious circle, because once you have had the experience of being impotent the worry that the same thing will happen again is enough to ensure that it does. So some men may become impotent over fairly long periods of time before regaining their potency.

Many young people have their first experience of impotence after drinking alcohol; and this may be completely unexpected, because alcohol tends to increase sexual desire and attraction and lower inhibitions.

Impotence can also occur *after* a man has achieved an erection, for example if he is having difficulty putting on a condom. He may then mistakenly think the fault lies with the condom and that it is not a suitable form of contraception for him. Or, whether he has a condom or not, it may suddenly feel as though he has lost contact with the vagina in the middle of intercourse. This is because the vagina widens as the woman becomes progressively excited, but the man may begin to doubt whether he is erect at all, and these doubts will make him lose his erection.

How should you tackle the problem of being impotent? First and foremost by not taking it, and yourself, too seriously: it is not a disaster. Probably, without knowing it, you have a lot of fellow-sufferers. Instead, try talking to your friends about the problem; admit your imperfections instead of boasting. They will probably take their courage in both hands and confess their own minor weaknesses. You may even find that by taking the initiative in this rather surprising way you have created a friendlier and healthier atmosphere in the class or at work.

When you find yourself impotent in a sexual situation, you should talk to the woman in the same way and tell her that it is quite a usual occurrence which will adjust itself again, possibly not today but another time. Once you have said this, you should not lie and wait for an erection, or allow her to feel at fault, but continue petting or do something else.

The woman, for her part, should accept the situation – and if she did not know it before, then she now knows that it is something which occurs to many young men. There are women who feel hurt by the man's impotence because they take it as a sign that he does not care for them or desire them enough. As we have said, nothing could be more mistaken. In fact the reason may well be that he cares too much.

The worst thing she can do is to show impatience, let alone contempt. This will naturally have the effect of bringing his impotence home to him. He cannot get an erection just by wanting to do so – the desire and will to achieve an erection may be so all-absorbing that it just won't happen.

If you have lost your erection after putting on a condom, there will obviously be a strong temptation to pull it off and take a chance without it. But it is more sensible to treat this kind of impotence in the same way as any other, and revert to petting, keeping the condom on.

If you have lost your erection during actual intercourse, then you should calmly begin again. If she was about to come when you broke off you could satisfy her by masturbation first. This will also relieve whatever feelings of guilt or incompetence the interruption has provoked in you and make it easier for you to overcome your impotence. In any case, continue caressing her until you feel your erection return.

There can, however, be more permanent forms of impotence, due either to psychological opposition between the lovers or to some deep-rooted aspect of the young man's adolescence. Only a psychiatrist or therapist will be able to help unravel the threads of this kind of problem.

Adjusting to each other

It can happen that even in a very loving relationship, conflict arises when one partner has a stronger sexual urge than the other. At no time is it more important to discuss your feelings and try to come to some sort of compromise. If one partner makes constant and unwelcome demands on the other, sex may soon change from being a shared pleasure to a source of recrimination and guilt.

No matter which partner is the more sexually active, the other partner's enjoyment of sex is bound to be affected. If a man is encouraged to 'perform' more often than he feels able, he is almost bound to feel inadequate, because most men have been brought up to believe that the man should be the sexual 'aggressor'. Such feelings of inadequacy may well lead to impotence, which makes the inequality of desire even worse.

A woman who is brought up to believe that sexual passivity is acceptable for women may initially accept, and even enjoy, the feeling of being 'swept off her feet'. In time, however, she will begin to find the constant demands burdensome. Often this results in a string of excuses: 'I've got a headache', 'I'm busy', 'we might wake the children'. If excuses replace real discussion sexual enjoyment will disappear, the man certain that his partner doesn't love him any more and the woman tensing up and rejecting every sexual advance.

It is not often that sexual desire is so out of proportion that it cannot be accommodated. Many people find that their sexual feelings go in cycles. This is particularly true of women, who often find that they feel 'turned on' at particular times in their menstrual cycles and not at others. If both partners understand this, it should not be too much to ask for one partner to 'lay off' during the times when his or her partner is not interested, in the anticipation that they'll have a far more enjoyable time together later on. If this seems impossible, the more active partner can always resort to masturbating when the urge seems too great.

It is not uncommon for people who feel that they have totally incompatible sex drives to look outside their primary relationship for other lovers. This may not be a good way to deal with the problem, because it would take almost superhuman understanding for the more passive partner not to feel inadequate and abandoned. This is not to say that multiple relationships are by definition a bad thing. But, if they are to work, they have got to be based on openness, understanding and honesty, not on the apparent shortcomings of one member of a pair.

If the inequality arises from something more than a cyclical change in desire or slightly different sexual needs, there may be a deeper problem. If for example one partner genuinely loses all sexual feelings for the other, then life is likely to be miserable for both partners. If this happens it may simply be a signal that your relationship has run its course and you have grown away from each other. Perhaps you would be happier if you abandon the sexual aspects of your friendship and cultivate the other things that are good about it; the end of sexual desire need not mean the end of a friendly relationship. Or it might be that one or other of the partners is suffering from a particular sexual difficulty which he or she has never been frank about. If this is the case, one of the books listed on p. 137 or a visit to a sex therapist might transform the situation. Sometimes sexual desire disappears for no obvious reason, and if you care for each other enough to want to find the reason why, you could contact the Marriage Guidance Council or the Family Planning Association, either of whom can refer you together to a counsellor.

Contraception

In modern society our sex lives are inextricably bound up with the question of how we are going to avoid unwanted children.

As soon as sexual maturity is reached, with production of semen in boys and ovulation in girls, it is possible for fertilization to take place during intercourse.

Superstitions

Some people think that so long as one partner is under a certain age – fifteen, for example – then the girl cannot become pregnant. But sexual maturity can be reached much earlier, and there is no such natural form of contraception. Nor is it true that you cannot become pregnant while you are breast-feeding a child. You can, even if you still haven't had your first period after birth. The risk is simply less great than it would otherwise be.

There is also a widespread misunderstanding that if a woman does not reach orgasm, then she is sure not to become pregnant. Equally mistaken is the belief that if the woman lies on top with the man underneath during intercourse this will give some special protection. Finally there are some people who think that a woman cannot become pregnant if she has been diagnosed by a doctor as having a retroverted womb (a womb tilted backwards) or if her abdomen has been exposed to X-rays as part of some examination.

It stands to reason that if there were any simple effective means of preventing pregnancy which came 'naturally' we would all use them and no one would have to spend thousands of pounds on research, and there wouldn't be any unwanted babies.

Going to a clinic

If you are considering or already having intercourse, it is sensible to get the best birth control advice you can. If you do not want to have children yet, it is very much your responsibility to use the facilities available to ensure that you don't get pregnant accidentally. Because an unwanted pregnancy primarily affects a woman, it is sensible for all women to investigate what kind of birth control suits them best. This is not to say that a boy has no responsibility in this matter. Certainly, of the contraceptives available without a doctor's prescription, the condom (which we discuss later) is the only really safe method. However, the most effective kinds of birth control have been developed for women to use, and they cannot be obtained without a visit to a doctor or clinic.

If you have a clinic near you, it may well be a better bet than your doctor. For a start the staff are trained to deal with all kinds of contraception so they are more likely to be able to offer you a choice. It might also be easier to discuss contraception with someone who hasn't looked after you since you were born!

You do not have to be married to go to a clinic, though you are supposed to be over sixteen to get contraceptives without your parents' permission. Don't let this put you off if you are younger; many clinics would rather turn a blind eye to your age than let you run the risk of becoming pregnant. If you feel embarrassed about going to a clinic on your own the first time, it may help to take a friend with you.

WHAT TO DO

The telephone number of the clinic is in the phone directory under 'Family Planning'. It is best to telephone or go round in advance to find out when the clinic is open and whether you have to make an appointment. Most clinics have appointment systems, and some have quite long waiting lists. If this is the case, and you don't feel you can wait that long, tell them that it's rather urgent and they will probably give you condoms and pessaries (see pp. 91–5) to tide you over. Don't forget that the clinic provides a completely free service including supplies. Once you've seen the cost of any kind of contraceptive in a chemist you will realize that this is another big advantage of using a clinic!

THE EXAMINATION

Probably the thing that puts most people off clinics is worry about the internal (vaginal) examination. It's sad that they should feel this way, because examinations are really no big deal. But still, if the only person who has ever seen your vagina is the person you make love with, it can seem a little strange to have a perfect stranger look and feel inside you.

Whatever kind of contraception you are eventually given, the doctor will always start by examining your vagina to make sure that you are healthy. To do this she has to insert something called a *speculum*, a scissor-shaped instrument with flat, slightly rounded blades. This is used to gently part the walls of your vagina so that the neck of your womb (the cervix) is visible. She will usually then take the speculum out and feel the shape of your uterus by putting two fingers inside you and her other hand on top.

This examination is quick and easy provided you are feeling relaxed. If you are very tense and nervous the muscles around your vagina will contract, and that makes it very hard to get anything inside at all (as you have probably discovered for yourself in other situations). If you remember that the doctor, who in a clinic is nearly always a woman, does dozens of these examinations every week it might help you to feel less personally embarrassed.

After the examination, the doctor will discuss with you the kinds of contraception available. If you read the rest of this chapter you should be in a very good position, with her advice, to make a well-informed decision about what you feel would suit you best.

Bad methods of contraception

ʻCOITUS INTERRUPTUS'

This is the method in which the man pulls his penis out of the vagina immediately before the ejaculation. This method has been known for thousands of years and used by many, including Onan as described in Genesis (see p. 38). But it has many drawbacks.

First of all it is very unsafe. The drops of fluid which come out of the penis to lubricate may contain active sperm cells which will be left in the vagina when the penis first enters it. Furthermore, before the final, large portion of semen comes – and so that you can't notice it – a small amount of lubrication also containing active sperm cells may be released. Besides, the semen is very often ejaculated on to the woman's outer sex organs, and since the sperm cells are mobile they may enter the vagina.

Not only is it an unsafe method, it is also very unsatisfying, because intercourse is broken off at the very time when it is by far the best. In terms of feeling, it can be shattering for a woman if she does not quite reach orgasm, but it isn't much fun for the man either. Altogether, any opportunity for feeling a sense of union is destroyed, and for many couples this may be as enriching a part of their relationship as the whole act. There will also be an increased risk of fertilization if any further intercourse is engaged upon, even if the man washes his penis and passes water in between.

So if the man promises to be really careful and means by this promise that he is going to break off intercourse, the woman should not feel completely safe – since it is in the nature of sex that he may not be able to keep his promise however much he wants to.

If you find yourself in a sexual situation and have no protective device with you – and this can happen to everyone – it is much safer to satisfy each other by petting than to use coitus interruptus, which is unsatisfactory both emotionally and as a contraceptive technique.

THE SAFE PERIOD (or rhythm method)

A woman is most likely to become pregnant if she has intercourse around the time of ovulation. For most women this is approximately midway between periods (about fourteen days before the start of the next period). After the egg has been released it can live inside the body for 12–24 hours. Sperm, once it has got into the uterus or fallopian tubes, can live up to five days. Adding these two factors together, it is clear that the days when you are most likely to conceive are those from five days before ovulation to two days afterwards. Adding on a couple more for security, then, the time of the month when you should *avoid* intercourse if you do not want to get pregnant is between nineteen and ten days before the start of the next period.

You can tell when you are ovulating by taking your temperature with a 'basal body temperature thermometer' every morning as soon as you wake up and before doing anything else. On the day of ovulation it will have fallen by between 0·2 and 0·4°F. Some women notice also that their cervical mucus (discharge) changes in texture at ovulation, becoming thinner and more copious. If you can pinpoint ovulation, you can be reasonably certain that from two days afterwards until the next period will be safe. However, unless you can predict with certainty when ovulation is going to occur, the days before ovulation are never really safe.

Although this is the only form of birth control officially allowed by the Catholic Church at the moment, I do not recommend the safe period method. The time of ovulation can vary slightly from month to month and may be influenced by many external factors, especially when you are young. Besides, now and then you may either want or have the opportunity to make love during just the nine days or so when you aren't allowed to, so that you become irritable with each other, or break the ban and take a chance. Finally, it would seem that there are some women for whom there simply is no 'safe period', and the only way you can find out if you are one of these is by getting pregnant.

DOUCHES

A douche is an instrument for squirting water into the vagina under mild pressure. They are used by some women to keep clean. This is not only unnecessary; it is harmful to the delicate balance of the vaginal fluids. Using a douche after intercourse is probably the most unsafe contraceptive method of all. Once the sperm cells have entered the cervix – and this can sometimes happen within one minute – they cannot be rinsed out. In fact the douche may easily push them faster into the womb.

SPERMICIDAL PESSARIES, CREAMS AND FOAMS

Pessaries are pushed up into the end of the vagina and left to dissolve in front of the entrance to the womb about ten minutes before you wish to have intercourse. Creams and foams are applied in the same way with the help of an applicator. These can all be obtained without a prescription from most chemists.

None of them is safe when used alone. However, if you have no alternative, foam is the best of the spermicides. If you do use it, be sure to shake the can vigorously (at least twenty times) before use, and use two full applicators. Add more if you have intercourse a second time. These products are much safer used in conjunction with a condom. They can also be used to increase the safety of the coil.

Reliable means of protection

THE CONDOM (PROTECTIVE, FRENCH LETTER, RUBBER, SHEATH)

The condom is a rubber sheath which is rolled down over the stiff penis like a fingerstall. Before you put it on, you can unroll the condom just a little to see which way it should be rolled on. Then you draw the foreskin back and slowly roll the condom down over the penis. If you rush it, you risk getting some of the rubber you have already rolled on stuck into rings – then you have to roll it back until it has come unstuck and lies smooth.

While you are putting it on try to make sure that no air gets in between the condom and the penis, since air bubbles have been known to cause the rubber to split. If the condom has a teat or sperm reservoir, twist the teat round a couple of times before you put the condom on. You must also be careful not to tear holes in the rubber with your fingernails.

You should put on your condom before actual intercourse, for the reasons we have listed above under 'coitus interruptus', otherwise safety is diminished. Besides, you may also find it difficult to put on the condom once the penis has become moist at the beginning of intercourse. In such cases you will find it easiest to dry yourself thoroughly before rolling the condom on.

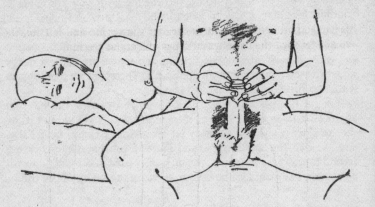

The foreskin is drawn back and the condom rolled slowly down over the penis.

You can buy both dry and lubricated condoms. The latter are a bit more expensive and slightly more difficult to put on, and they slip off more easily; but they are less likely to tear. The lubrication also compensates for the penis's natural lubrication, so they feel more 'natural'. If you use unlubricated condoms you can smear a little contraceptive cream or KY Jelly (both stocked by chemists) on the outside of the condom when you have rolled it on. You can use saliva at a pinch, but don't use other forms of lubrication as they may irritate the woman's vagina.

When intercourse is over and the semen has been released into the condom, it can easily slip off if you carry on moving or wait until the penis is limp again before you withdraw. So the most sensible thing is to withdraw immediately after orgasm, holding the condom in place with a couple of fingers while you do so. This way you can also establish quite early on whether the condom is still in one piece. If it has burst, apply more spermicide if you have any, and look under 'morning after methods' (p. 104).

Some people think that it is safer to put on two condoms at once. It isn't; on the contrary the two condoms may easily rub each other to pieces during the movements of intercourse.

When the used condom has been drawn off, the penis will be

covered in a wet layer of semen which both partners may get on their fingers if love play is continued. The semen can be conveyed from the fingers to the woman's sex organs and from there the sperm cells may be able to travel into the vagina. So if you are going to continue love play, it is advisable for the man to wash his penis and his hands thoroughly – he might even pass water as well – so that the remains of the semen are washed away from the urethra.

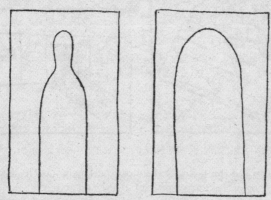

Left and right: a condom with and without a teat.

Before you embark on intercourse again, you should have a new condom on. If you haven't any more with you, then you will have to make do with petting. Or you could wash the used condom thoroughly on both sides, dry it and inflate it to the size of a milk-bottle. You should then hold the inflated condom up to a strong light and examine it carefully for tears, finally powdering it with talcum powder or something similar. Then the condom can be rolled up and will be ready to use again. Most good condoms will stand up to this treatment, but don't try it too often.

Condoms can be bought in chemists, in 'rubber goods' shops and in many barbers. They are also available from slot machines, usually in public lavatories. You can get them free from family planning clinics (women are often given packs containing both condoms and spermicidal pessaries). In addition, they can be obtained by mail order from the Family Planning Association and other distributors, and can be sent either to your home or 'poste restante' to the nearest post office.

Prices vary. The more expensive ones are usually the safest; if you buy cheaper ones make sure that they have 'BSI' (British Standards Institution) stamped on the box, which proves that they have been properly tested. If you are asked what size you want, the reference

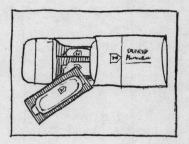

Two samples of wrapped condoms.

is to the size of the box *not* the condom, which only comes in one size.

A condom does not give complete protection even when it is correctly used, because it can tear or perish. It is between 80 and 97 per cent safe: that is, out of every 100 women using this method, between three and twenty get pregnant each year. If you want to increase safety you can use condoms in combination with spermicidal pessaries, creams and foams or with a diaphragm. A combination of this kind is particularly suitable during the nine days of possible

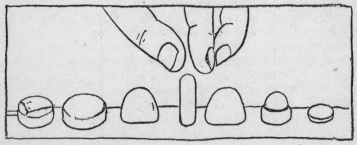

Examples of spermicidal pessaries.

ovulation (see pp. 89–90) if you do not want to risk having a child on any account.

Although condoms can nowadays be bought so discreetly that even the shyest person should be able to overcome his embarrassment, statistics show that many young people fuck without any kind of contraceptive. There are several reasons for this, and one of them is that young men do not make the effort to get themselves a packet of condoms.

If it became common practice for young boys of fourteen or fifteen onwards to buy themselves a few packets and practise using them during masturbation, they would be able to avoid many unwanted pregnancies later on. If you are masturbating in any case, you might just as well learn how to put on a condom properly so that you will be prepared when it matters.

Furthermore, it would be practical if both girls and boys made it a habit always to have one or two condoms with them. Condoms suitable for this purpose are those specially packed in individual, air-tight containers designed to protect them so that they won't be damaged by lying in a pocket or handbag for some length of time.

DIAPHRAGM (DUTCH CAP)

The diaphragm is a small rubber 'bowl' with a flexible metal ring round the edge. It is always used with some kind of spermicidal cream. The cream is spread round the outer edge and a blob is left

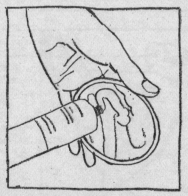

Contraceptive cream and diaphragm.

A. The first time you insert a diaphragm, it is wise to locate the cervix first, so that you know how far up it actually is. So explore first with a finger. Right at the end of your vagina you will find a lump, rather like the end of your nose, with a dimple in it.

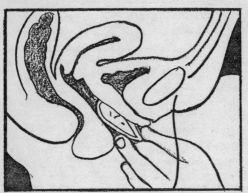

B. The diaphragm is now squeezed together and ready to be inserted.

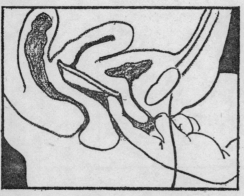

C. Push the diaphragm right to the end of the vagina so that the top edge sits in the hollow behind the cervix. Then push the nearest edge forwards and upwards with your fingers, so that the diaphragm is held in position by the back of the pubic bone.

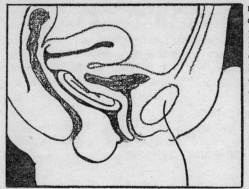

D. This shows the diaphragm incorrectly placed. This can happen if you do not push the diaphragm right up behind the cervix, but under it instead. As you can see, the cervix is then unprotected, allowing the semen access to the mouth of the womb.

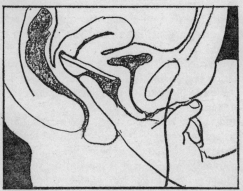

E. After you have inserted the diaphragm, check with a finger that you can feel the cervix through the soft rubber dome of the diaphragm.

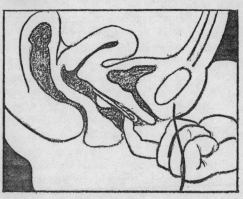

F. Take the diaphragm out – at least six hours after you last had intercourse by putting your finger up along the front wall of the vagina and grasping hold of the front edge of the diaphragm. Then pull it slowly and carefully.

in the middle on both sides of the rubber. The diaphragm is then inserted into the vagina as shown and described in the illustration, though it can be put in place with a specially made applicator.

Used correctly a diaphragm affords the same amount of protection against pregnancy as a condom: it is between 80 and 97 per cent safe. If you want to be absolutely sure it may be advisable to use both a diaphragm and a condom during the nine or so especially risky days between two periods.

If you have intercourse several times during the course of an evening you will need to insert a pessary or a new blob of cream (for which you need an applicator) on the front side of the diaphragm before each new coitus.

Before inserting a diaphragm, the bladder should be empty. Then you should take the diaphragm and smear the contraceptive cream on it. Next you stand with one foot on a chair (or squat), squeeze the diaphragm together between your fingers and you are ready to push it up into the vagina.

If you have a regular boyfriend, get him to try inserting it in you. This is one way of sharing responsibility for contraception, and it also makes insertion feel more like part of your love-making rather than an unwelcome bother.

The diaphragm should not be taken out until at least six hours after the last time you had intercourse. It should then be washed, dried and held up to the light while you draw the rubber slightly taut towards the metal ring to make sure that it is not torn in any way; then it should be powdered with talcum. You should never douche with a diaphragm in place, nor is it necessary after taking it out.

Unlike condoms, which will fit any man, a diaphragm can only be given to a girl after her vagina has been measured. You can be measured at a family planning clinic or at one of the clinics specially set up for young people. At a family planning clinic all consultation and supplies are free. You can buy the cream at a chemist without a prescription if you run out.

Since the vagina grows during puberty and afterwards, it is wise to have your measurements checked every six months or so. Similarly, new measurements must be taken after giving birth or having an abortion.

Since rubber rots slightly after a time, you should always change your diaphragm once a year. You can do this without a prescription at most chemists as long as you know which number to ask for, or take the old one with you, but you would have to pay for it, so it would be sensible to combine a change of cap with a visit to the clinic.

Any girl of sixteen or over can be measured for a diaphragm *without* her parents' permission. Before a doctor will take the measurements, however, the girl's hymen must be broken and the entrance to the vagina more or less unblocked. For most girls this means that they cannot get a diaphragm until they have had some experience of intercourse – and this is undeniably a disadvantage.

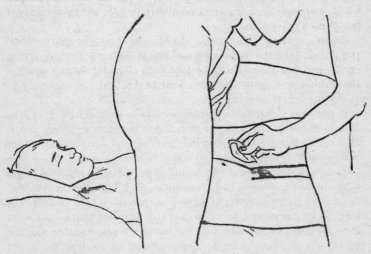

Putting in a diaphragm.

One advantage of the diaphragm over the condom is that you can insert it several hours before you expect to have intercourse and can then insert a pessary or cream in front of it shortly before intercourse. As a rule, neither partner will notice it is there during intercourse. So if you are going to a party where you think you may be drinking, it is safer to have put the diaphragm in your vagina than in your handbag. It isn't the slightest bit silly to be as careful as this, and there's nothing degrading about going home again *without* having made use of this kind of protection.

It is at those times when you are becoming sexually excited by dancing with someone or caressing them, and at the same time your inhibitions and common sense are diminishing under the influence of alcohol, that 'accidents' happen.

CERVICAL CAP

This kind of cap is made in the shape of a smaller but deeper bowl than an ordinary diaphragm. It is either made out of fairly stiff rubber with a metal edge or formed out of one piece of stiff plastic. It is put over the cervix like a hat, but it is not in common use because it is very difficult for the woman to put it correctly in place herself. When smeared with spermicidal cream and correctly positioned, it gives excellent protection as long as you do not leave it inside you any longer than you would an ordinary diaphragm. So if for some reason a woman cannot use an ordinary diaphragm, the pill or a coil, she might well look into the possibilities of a cervical cap.

THE INTRAUTERINE DEVICE (IUD, THE COIL, THE LOOP)

The coil is a little plastic gadget which is inserted through the cervix and can prevent what may be a fertilized egg from embedding itself in the membrane of the womb and developing into a foetus. The coil must only be inserted by a doctor, and it can remain in place for two or three years before being changed. This method is most suitable for women who have had a baby or an abortion because the cervix is slightly wider, although small coils have been developed which can be inserted in women who have never been pregnant.

The main advantage of the coil is that once it is in place you are protected all the time and don't have to remember to take a pill or put something inside you. Some women do experience side-effects with the coil; for instance it tends to increase menstrual bleeding and cramps. These effects often wear off after a few months, but if they are really bad the coil can always be removed by a doctor.

This method is not 100 per cent safe; approximately three out of every hundred women using it in a year are likely to get pregnant. If pregnancy does occur it is important to see a doctor quickly, because in a high percentage of such pregnancies the coil will cause a miscarriage, which is in itself quite an unpleasant experience and may also be accompanied by infection. If the coil is removed early in pregnancy the chances of such complications are reduced. If you do continue the pregnancy with the coil in place and you do not miscarry, it is not likely that the foetus will be harmed by the presence of the coil in your womb.

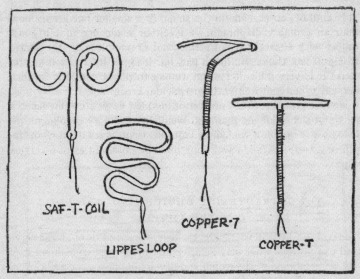

The coil, showing the different shapes available.

To be really safe it may be a good idea to use spermicide or a condom as well as the coil during your most fertile days.

THE CONTRACEPTIVE PILL

The pill gives almost complete protection against pregnancy so long as you take it according to the manufacturer's or the clinic's directions. It works by preventing ovulation, which must take place before an egg can be fertilized.

You can only get the pill with a prescription from a doctor, who before issuing it should give you a thorough check-up to make sure that you are not suffering from any of the diseases which can be aggravated by the pill. You should also be checked over every six months while you are using this form of contraception, and that check-up should, at the very least, include a blood pressure test.

The pill comes in packs of twenty to twenty-two. The manufacturer's instructions will advise you to start taking them once a day from the fifth day of your period, and to use another form of contraception in addition until you finish the first pack of pills. The Family Planning Association advise you to start the pills on the first day of your period, and they say that you do not need additional protection in the first month. Both lots of advice are equally good, and anyway after the first month the routine is always the same: once you have finished a pack of pills you wait for seven days and then start a new pack. In the 'off' time you will have a period, which is usually lighter and shorter than usual.

If you have forgotten to take the pill in the evening, you can catch up again the following morning. But if there is a gap of more than thirty-six hours between taking two pills there is a danger of ovula-

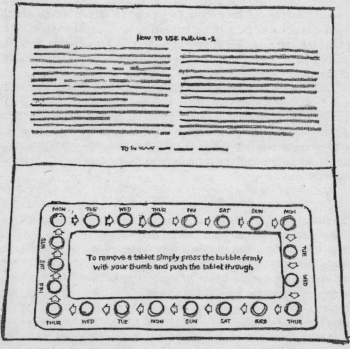

A packet of contraceptive pills.

tion taking place. So if you have forgotten to take your pills for more than thirty-six hours, you should continue to take them until the pack is finished, but you will also have to protect yourself with some other form of contraception and then start with the next pack five days after you have begun your period in the usual way.

It can be quite difficult to remember to take a pill every evening. Have a good think about it and put the pack in some place where you are bound to 'fall over it' every day, on your pillow, perhaps, or with your toothbrush. Obviously it is most difficult if you don't want your parents to know and have to hide the pack every time you take one.

You may find that you have forgotten to take the pills with you when you go away, for a weekend with friends, for example, and be tempted to borrow a couple from a girlfriend. But if you don't keep to the same brand for the entire twenty-one days you run the risk of ovulation taking place, because the different brands contain different quantities of hormones. To be on the safe side, you should again use another form of contraception while continuing with the pills. The same applies if you have been suffering from vomiting and/or diarrhoea since you cannot be sure that the pill has remained in the system long enough to be absorbed.

The first month you take the pill you may be bothered by nausea and feel generally unwell. These troubles should disappear if you continue taking the pill. If these symptoms are really nasty see your doctor, who can prescribe another brand after your period. It may be a question of not being able to take the particular combination of hormones selected by one manufacturer, while another will give you no trouble at all.

Another possible side-effect of the pill is that you may put on weight. This may be particularly bothersome if you were plump in the first place. The increase in weight is chiefly due to the fact that the pill causes the body to retain more liquid (as it does during pregnancy). Thus some people will combine the pill with tablets intended to expel the liquid again, but this is really going a bit far. You can keep your weight down without using artificial or dangerous means by keeping a watchful eye on your diet. If you wear contact lenses, the increase in fluid may change the shape and sensitivity of your eyes, and you might have to give up either the lenses or the pill.

Some women find also that the pill makes them feel tired, depressed or makes them lose interest in sex. Of course everyone can suffer from these problems sometimes, and it would be wrong to blame every 'down' in life on the pill. However, if you feel that your mood has altered for no obvious reason since you started the pill, try some other kind of contraception for a while to find out whether the pill is to blame.

There are some diseases, such as diabetes and liver disease, which are aggravated by the pill. Women suffering from them should either avoid the pill altogether or use it only under strict supervision. It now seems certain also that women on the pill who are over thirty-five run an increased risk of blood clots, heart disease and other 'circulatory' problems. Women with a history of such diseases in their family, particularly if they smoke, are most at risk. It is certainly not wise to stay on the pill for more than five years at a stretch, so it would be wrong to regard it as a permanent method of contraception. However, for younger women, provided they don't suffer from any of the problems listed above, risks from the pill appear to be small; certainly they are less than the risk of pregnancy. But it probably wouldn't be wise to start the pill until your periods are well established.

On the positive side, the pill can improve the complexion, reduce heavy menstrual bleeding and get rid of period cramps; and for some women the added weight is not unwelcome.

MORNING AFTER METHODS

Generally speaking, if you have had intercourse without protection, or if you have had an accident with a condom, there is nothing that can be done after the event. However, in some areas, clinics are prepared to provide 'morning after' pills or IUDs. The 'morning after' pill contains, in a very high dosage, some of the ingredients of ordinary contraceptive pills. It is certainly not advisable to use this method more than once, and it does have unpleasant side-effects such as nausea and diarrhoea. The 'morning after' IUD is in fact the same as any IUD. As long as it is inserted before the foetus implants in the womb it will operate quite normally, preventing the implantation of this egg (if it was in fact fertilized). The advantage of this last-ditch method is that, unlike the pill, the IUD will stay inside you and continue to give you protection.

If you want to try for either of these methods you must get to a clinic within 72 hours of the possible conception. It is most important not to leave it any later, because not only will it not work, it may also cause damage to the foetus (in the case of the pill) or a septic miscarriage (in the case of the IUD).

One other method of invervening after conception is 'menstrual extraction'. This method is usually classified as an abortion (as the two methods above could be), and it is not yet widely available in this country because of the abortion laws. If and when it does become available it could be a tremendous step forward as a back-up method of contraception. In menstrual extraction, a doctor puts a fine tube up into the uterus and extracts the contents by vacuum. This can be done at the time of the expected period or up to eighteen days afterwards. It is not 100 per cent certain that the method will work; occasionally it has to be repeated.

The future

Scientific research continues to explore new methods of contraception, just as there are still attempts to improve existing ones.

One method under examination is the use of a chemical called 'prostaglandin'. This substance, when produced naturally in the body, triggers off contractions in childbirth. It may also be responsible for menstrual cramps. Used artificially, it can start labour in childbirth and late abortion. It may be possible to use it in much smaller quantities, very early in pregnancy, so that the foetus would be expelled before it implanted in the womb.

Some much smaller-scale research is currently being done into 'barrier' methods, like the cap. It may be possible to design a barrier which could be worn inside the vagina for days at a time without causing irritation or infection. Such a method would be of particular benefit to women, as it would have none of the side-effects of the more sophisticated methods.

INJECTABLE CONTRACEPTIVES

Contraceptive injections are being tested in some parts of this country and elsewhere. The injections contain similar ingredients to the contraceptive pill but because they are long-lasting (three to six months) the dose cannot be adjusted to get rid of irritating side-effects; you just have to put up with them until the effect of the injection wears off. It is wise to avoid injectables until the time (if ever) when they have been fully tested and found to be free of side-effects as well as safe.

Abortion or birth

The first signs of pregnancy

If menstruation fails to take place or is very weak and lasts only a short time, possibly with the blood a more brownish colour than usual, it may be a sign that you are pregnant. But you may have a late period or miss one altogether without necessarily being pregnant. Fear of pregnancy alone can disrupt the menstrual cycle.

Nausea, morning sickness, general malaise and tiredness can be early signs of pregnancy, but may also be the outward expression of pregnancy fears. A feeling of tightness in the breasts, however, almost always follows conception.

Twelve to fourteen days after the day on which your period was due it is possible to confirm pregnancy fairly reliably with a urine test. This can be done by your doctor, at a family planning clinic or at a chemist. If you want more anonymity, you can send a sample of your urine either to the British Pregnancy Advisory Service (see p. 135) or to one of the commercial testing laboratories which advertise in many magazines and on public transport.

About four weeks after the missed period it should be possible for a doctor to tell whether you are pregnant by examination. So if your test proves negative and your period still doesn't come you should see a doctor; some tests give false negatives. Whatever you want to do about your pregnancy, it is important to see a doctor early to get the medical care that you will need.

What is an abortion?

By abortion we mean the termination of the pregnancy before the foetus is viable or capable of independent life. Practically speaking the foetus must be under seven months old. A normal pregnancy lasts about nine months, though some births take place between the seventh and ninth month, in which case they are called 'premature' births since the baby has a good chance of survival.

Spontaneous abortion (miscarriage)

Abortion can occur spontaneously if the womb cannot retain the foetus for some reason and expels it before time. Most spontaneous abortions, or miscarriages, take place during the first three months of pregnancy. The earlier they occur, the more difficult it is to distinguish them from a heavy period. It is therefore acknowledged that many spontaneous abortions take place without the woman knowing that she had been pregnant. If there is any reason to suppose that you have had a spontaneous abortion it is sensible to go to a doctor, since it may be necessary to scrape the womb to remove the remains of the membrane surrounding the foetus and the placenta. This scraping, or curettage, takes place in a hospital. About 10 per cent of pregnancies end in this way.

Induced abortion

It is also possible to have an abortion done by a doctor to end a pregnancy which is unwanted for social or health reasons. The majority of these abortions are done in the first three months of pregnancy by a method in which a tube is put into your womb and the contents drawn out by suction. In later pregnancy, it is usual for a doctor to introduce a chemical into the womb which causes you to expel the foetus just as you would in labour. Most women and medical staff find late abortions upsetting, which makes it particularly important for you to seek advice early if you think an abortion will be necessary.

Legal abortion

Until 1967 abortion was illegal in Britain. This meant that those women who could afford to pay high prices for illegal operations were able to get safe abortions, and those who could not either had to bear unwanted children or resorted to 'back-street' abortionists. Though sometimes well-meaning, these abortionists were not trained, operations took place in unsterile conditions and often ended in tragedy.

It is thought that between 50,000 and 150,000 illegal abortions took place every year until the Abortion Act was passed in 1967. This Act states that an abortion can be carried out if two doctors agree that (a) there would be more risk to the physical or mental health of the mother or her existing children if the pregnancy were continued than if it were terminated, or (b) there is substantial risk of the baby being born seriously handicapped. In practice, this is interpreted very differently by different doctors. Some believe that every woman should have the right to decide whether she wants to continue a pregnancy; others believe that abortion is acceptable only in very extreme cases.

Since 1967 it has become very much easier to get a safe legal abortion in Britain, but it is still much more difficult in some areas than in others. The reason for this is that some senior gynaecologists (doctors specializing in women's diseases) are against abortion, and they use their influence to stop abortions being done in their hospitals. In addition the government has put too little money into setting up abortion clinics. This has meant that those doctors who are willing to help are unable to cope with the numbers of patients coming to them. In fact only about half of all abortions done in Britain are carried out free in National Health hospitals.

For this reason, two charities were set up to give assistance to women living in areas where they could not get help. They are the Pregnancy Advisory Service, which is in London, and the British

Pregnancy Advisory Service, which has branches all over the country. There will probably be one near enough for you to get help if you should need it. Neither of these charities provides free services, but they keep their costs as low as possible and will always provide financial aid to women who cannot find the money to pay. Their addresses are on pp. 135–6.

A word of warning; there are also a number of other pregnancy bureaux (some with very similar names to the ones above) which are commercial and often charge high prices for an inferior service. There is also an organization called Lifeline, which advertises widely, particularly in railway stations. This service is dedicated to persuading women not to have abortions, and is better avoided unless you are certain that abortion is not for you, in which case they may give you help in other ways.

Is abortion safe?

Although most women expect to become pregnant at some time in their lives, every pregnancy carries with it some element of risk. It is best to use contraception and avoid getting pregnant if you don't want to have a baby. However, if an abortion is carried out in the first three months of pregnancy it is, in statistical terms, safer than actually having a baby, and there is little risk of serious after-effects. In a few cases, infection gets into the womb during or after the abortion, and this can cause serious problems if it is not treated quickly by a doctor.

Illegal or self-induced abortion is a different matter. Some people think that you can bring on a miscarriage by jumping up and down, taking laxatives, contraceptive or other pills, drinking gin and a number of other things. If the foetus is not going to dislodge naturally none of these things will work. If what you take is poisonous it might also make you ill and could easily affect the foetus. So if you have swallowed anything in an attempt to cause a miscarriage you should tell a doctor.

Basically any method of abortion which is not medically approved and carried out by a trained person is likely to be very dangerous; so if you are pregnant you should see a doctor.

Some people make much of the effect of abortion on the mind. A certain amount of regret is quite normal, but it is unlikely to persist if you have made a clear decision in your own mind that abortion is right in your circumstances. It is important not to get pushed into having an abortion if you don't want one. This may be the first major decision of your life, and though you may feel insecure and afraid it is one of those decisions which you must make for yourself in the end.

What to do

If you suspect that you are pregnant, you may feel tempted to ignore it in the hopes that 'something will happen'. You may find it impossible to believe that you are pregnant. Unfortunately it is extremely unlikely that 'something will happen' and pregnancy can quite easily happen to any woman, so it is important to do something about it, no matter how afraid you feel. The best first step is to get a pregnancy test two weeks after the expected date of your period (see p. 107). If it is negative the relief may bring your period on. If it doesn't, you should have another test a week later. If it is still negative but your period hasn't come, it is wise to see a doctor anyway; some people always show up negative. And don't stop using contraception in the meantime.

If your test is positive, don't keep the information to yourself; it will help to discuss it all with someone you trust. Many girls are afraid to tell their parents about a pregnancy, but it is important to remember that if you are under sixteen one of them would have to sign a consent form before you could have an abortion, and if you don't have an abortion they will soon find out just by looking that you are pregnant. However strict and disapproving parents may appear to be when they are discussing other people's daughters 'getting into trouble', when it is their own daughter they will usually do all they can to help.

If you decide, after discussing all the pro's and cons, that an abortion would be the best action, you should go to your own doctor. If he or she is unsympathetic, or doesn't think that the hospital will be helpful, you can go to one of the pregnancy advisory services mentioned above (pp. 109–10).

Once you have been referred for an abortion you will have to go into a clinic or hospital for anything between six hours and three days, according to their practice and your needs. If you are less than about four months pregnant, you will be offered a general anaesthetic, which sends you to sleep so you won't feel anything. If you are later than that you will have a chemical introduced into your womb, usually through a tube. This will start labour; the abortion will take several hours and will be painful.

After the abortion you can expect light bleeding (like period bleeding) for a few days. If the bleeding is heavy, if you have any pain, or start running a temperature you should contact your doctor. It may be a sign of infection, which can usually be cured with medication, or that the abortion wasn't finished properly and will need to be done again.

Adoption

Some women feel that even if a pregnancy was unplanned and unwanted and it would be impossible to bring up a child, abortion is out of the question. Others try to conceal their pregnancies or are unaware of them until it is too late to do anything, and an unlucky few are unable to get the help they need early in pregnancy.

If you are going to go ahead with the pregnancy, it is important to talk to someone older who has experience of bringing up children so that you will have a clear understanding of the options ahead of you. Child care is a full-time responsibility, and unless you feel absolutely ready for it, it is unwise, both for your own future and for your child's, to attempt it.

Giving up a baby can be very hard but there are many people who are unable to have children of their own and will be overjoyed to have a baby to adopt. If you do decide that this is the best thing to do, you should get things organized before the baby is born. Most local authorities can arrange adoption, so contact your social services department. They will put you in touch with a social worker who will help you make the arrangements. If this is not possible where you live, you can go straight to an adoption society. If you have made these arrangements in advance, the baby can be sent to foster parents after the birth, until the adoption is arranged (which won't take very long). If fostering is not arranged, you will be expected to take care of the baby yourself. He or she will be officially your responsibility until the adoption papers are signed.

If you haven't made up your mind about adoption, no one can take your baby away (unless of course you ill-treat it). Even if you've already made arrangements with an adoption society, you cannot be forced to give up your child. He or she is yours until you sign the adoption papers. However, the sooner the baby is with the people who are going to bring it up, the sooner it will settle down and adjust to them. So try to make an honest assessment in advance. Don't keep the baby if you aren't going to be able to cope.

Sexual
alternatives

Our sexual feelings are a combination of physical and emotional needs. The physical response cycle (described on pp. 69–73) is basically the same for everyone, but the stimulation and emotion that trigger off those responses vary considerably. In pre-revolutionary China foot-binding was common, and the bound foot was considered very erotic; other people enjoy wearing, or watching others wearing, strange clothing; and the western male's obsession with breasts would be considered quirky in many parts of Africa, where bottoms are considered far more erotic.

It isn't easy either to understand what it is that attracts people to each other. Women are not always drawn to big brawny men, nor men to shy gentle women, although this model of behaviour is the one which is most often presented as normal. In fact even with a close friend we may find it impossible to understand why he or she is attracted to a certain person, and wonder what on earth they see in one another. Our needs vary; we may be drawn to someone who is similar in temperament or totally different, we may feel closer to someone who is much older or much younger than ourselves or to someone of the same or the opposite sex, and our needs may change with experience.

Our behaviour is not only conditioned by the feelings which have grown up in our minds; it is also affected by society's expectations. Sometimes the two may be in total conflict so that we suppress our real feelings, which may then 'bubble up' in forms of sexual expression that are actually harmful; or we may express our frustration by condemning the pleasure of others. People who decide to express feelings which are not in line with those expectations often face not only disapproval but prison sentences.

In the broadest terms, our society shows approval for sexual relationships which lead to marriage and the reproduction of the traditional family unit. Therefore a woman who is too old to have children is disapproved of if she enters a relationship with a young man, whereas an older man who marries a young woman is tolerated. Relationships outside marriage and homosexual relationships are also seen as a threat to this ideal family unit and are therefore taboo.

Sexual taboos have varied throughout history and from one society to another. In ancient Greece, male homosexuality was seen as a higher form of love than heterosexual unions; in some societies sexual initiation by older people is traditional; multiple marriages are a sign of status in some countries although they are illegal in Britain. Rules and regulations have little to do with sexual expression, but they have forced sections of the population to hide their feelings, expressing them in secret or not at all. Many people are now beginning to realize that condemnation of particular forms of sexual behaviour is oppressive not only because it forces many people to lead a life of guilt and fear but also because it prevents people from exploring their own sexuality for fear of discovering that something is 'wrong' with them.

However, although attitudes to sexual behaviour are growing more liberal, prejudice is still firmly embedded in the fabric of our society. As we explain on p. 46, homosexuality is still treated with suspicion, and in some countries (including Scotland and Northern Ireland) it is actually illegal. In a world which really respected our right to sexual freedom, the law would not intervene except to prevent people from imposing their sexuality on others by force.

Two of the strongest taboos in our society are those against incest and sex with children (paedophilia). Both of these taboos are backed up by the law.

Incest

By this we mean sexual relations between adults and their children or grandchildren and between brothers and sisters. Sexual intercourse between such close relatives is illegal in most countries, though in some cultures it used to be allowed during certain religious ceremonies.

The incest taboo is probably the strongest of all the rules which govern our sexual behaviour. Initially the reasons for it were probably to ensure that different family groups made and maintained relationships with one another through marriage. This on the one hand encouraged cooperation rather than antagonism between groups and on the other hand prevented in-breeding. If in-breeding had been widespread the human race would probably not have survived, because it tends to weaken each successive generation by duplicating things like bad eyesight or deafness, rather than counteracting them with the characteristics of another family.

Paedophilia

Paedophiles are people who are emotionally and sexually drawn to children. Such a method of sexual satisfaction is generally considered indecent and harmful to children and is punishable by prison sentences.

Usually these people are kind and gentle to children. They rarely try to have intercourse and are usually satisfied with mutual caressing. In fact, a paedophile is no more likely than any other person to use force to achieve sexual satisfaction. He or she relies on the natural sexual curiosity of most children. Some children find warmth and support in these relationships which they don't get elsewhere; but nevertheless a relationship of this kind is based on inequality. An adult inevitably has power over a child because of his or her greater age and experience, and a child cannot really freely consent to such a relationship.

Such early relationships are not necessarily harmful but the atmosphere of guilt and fear which inevitably surrounds an activity which is regarded with total abhorrence by the majority of people must have some effect on a child's future sexual behaviour. So it is probably best that children should be warned not to go with strangers, even if they are offered presents.

Transvestites

Transvestites are people who have a strong desire to wear the clothes of the opposite sex. Some are also homosexual. A few transvestites do not feel it satisfying simply to change clothes; they feel they belong to the wrong sex, and wish to change sex. These are called 'transsexuals', and some of them actually change sex by means of special operations and hormone treatments.

Exhibitionists and Peeping Toms (*voyeurs*)

Exhibitionists are men who feel a desire to expose their genitals in public places. Peeping Toms are men who get sexual stimulation out of secretly watching people undressing or making love. In neither case is it likely that they would actually harm the other people; in fact they are usually too frightened themselves to do anything but run away if challenged. Nevertheless, their behaviour is both an invasion of privacy and a source of fear for many women.

An exhibitionist usually hides somewhere and then steps out in front of some unsuspecting woman exposing his penis. If the woman is frightened, the fear will give him an erection and this is what he wants. If the woman remains calm or speaks to him, he will probably run away. Although it is unpleasant to be imposed on in this way there is no need to be frightened, as exhibitionists are usually both impotent in normal sexual situations and pretty timid.

Peeping at couples making love is an activity which has always been condoned in certain situations: blue movies and porn magazines make a great deal of money exploiting the fact that many people get a thrill out of watching other people having sex. Even such commercial peeping is exploitative because it fosters a belief that women are sexual objects rather than human beings, and it concentrates on sex as a purely physical act totally divorced from the caring and warmth of loving relationships.

Some people take this kind of 'turn on' even further and haunt back alleys and gardens hoping for a glimpse of someone else's sex life. If the watched is not aware of the watcher little harm has been done, but sooner or later the peeper gets bolder, climbs on window-sills, presses his face to the window and gets noticed. When this happens, the fear and unease which such behaviour can cause cannot be dismissed, even though peepers rarely do more than peep.

Sometimes behaviour which in a milder form would simply be a 'quirk' turns into an obsession which is a danger to others. There are some people who get stimulation out of frightening or hurting others. It is not easy to understand how an act which for most people is an expression of love can become for others so closely tied to pain and violence. Clearly nobody has the right to ill-treat another person for their own satisfaction, no matter how strongly they feel compelled to do so.

Sadism and masochism

A sadist is a person who can only be sexually stimulated by hurting another person, and a masochist is a person who has to be hurt to achieve the same result. Quite often a person can be a sadist and a masochist at the same time.

Many people show streaks of sadism or masochism in their love play, and so long as this is acceptable to both partners it can hardly be called anti-social. For some people, however, such behaviour becomes a necessary pre-condition for sexual stimulation or satis-faction and in this case it is but a small step from rough love play to a real desire to hurt the other person.

Rape

Rape is what occurs when a man forces a woman to have intercourse against her will. Rape is a crime which is always humiliating, often violent and almost always psychologically damaging to some degree. The majority of rapes take place between people who are known to each other, not, as many people believe, between strangers in dark alleys. The right to say no is a right which should be respected in any situation, but unfortunately this is not always the case. There is a widely held assumption that a woman who appears to encourage a man sexually is 'asking for it'. In some cases encouragement can be seen as simply asking for a lift, wearing 'provocative' clothing, or inviting a man home for coffee.

The crime of rape is a product of a society in which male sexual aggression is encouraged and considered normal. While children are brought up to believe that 'no' means 'yes' when a woman says it, and that all women secretly yearn to be dominated, women will continue to be forced into sexual intercourse against their will.

Of course the 'dark alley' rapes do occur; in fact they are on the increase and as women become more independent they are more likely to find themselves alone in dangerous situations. While the threat of rape should not be a reason to curtail independence it is wise for women to take certain precautions: avoiding hitchhiking alone at night; try to keep to lighted streets rather than unlit shortcuts; help each other by arranging to go home in a group if you are going to be out late at night.

Some women are learning self-defence and find that just the knowledge that they can defend themselves gives a tremendous boost to their confidence. Nonetheless, if you are attacked, don't fight back unless you are pretty certain you can get away, or you may be encouraging greater violence. Similarly, if you know there are people near enough to hear, shout 'help' or 'fire' (screaming often goes unnoticed these days), but if there is no one around it is probably safer in the end to be completely passive. By behaving totally calmly some women have even managed to talk a man out of it.

If you have been raped and would like to talk to someone about the emotional, physical or legal repercussions, there are now rape crisis centres in several cities (see p. 136).

Prostitution and pornography

Prostitutes are people who have sex with others for money. Pornography is showing sex in pictures or text for the purpose of sexual stimulation. The similarity between this is that in both cases sexuality is used for making money.

PROSTITUTION

Most prostitutes are women, sometimes called whores, though there are male prostitutes too. The vast majority of clients of prostitutes are male. When prostitutes share a house or other establishment it is then called a brothel. In some countries brothels are run openly; sometimes they are even controlled by the government, but in Britain brothels are illegal.

Most prostitutes get their clients by 'soliciting' (approaching men in the street and offering themselves). That is also illegal in this country and prostitutes are regularly rounded up by police; after three such 'offences' they can be sent to prison. Their clients are not acting against the law. To avoid the police, many women operate through advertisements, massage parlours and escort agencies. This is also technically 'soliciting' and still illegal, but as long as women don't advertise themselves openly as prostitutes they are usually safe from the law.

It is illegal for any third person (a 'pimp') to live off the earnings of a prostitute or to help a prostitute find clients, but it is not actually illegal for anyone to receive money themselves for sex.

The confusing legal situation is a reflection of society's confused attitude on prostitution. Men have never been punished for using prostitutes, and yet women are punished for being used as prostitutes. Society cannot make its mind up whether prostitution is a social necessity for sexually deprived men (sexually deprived women have never been similarly catered for) or an evil which should be stamped out. Probably if women had access to more interesting and better-paid work, and if social security payments for single parents were higher, very few women would turn to prostitution for their keep. In the meantime women's prisons are full of prostitutes.

Prostitutes inevitably run the risk of contracting venereal disease and for this reason they usually ask their clients to use condoms. It is, however, wise to visit a VD clinic after sex with a prostitute.

PORNOGRAPHY

Pornography has long been the subject of angry controversy. Some people think that it should be banned altogether in case it leads young people astray; many feminists oppose it because of the way in which women are portrayed as sex objects to gratify male desires.

Some people think that pictures which arouse sexual appetites by portraying women being attacked or humiliated actually cause sex crimes by making people think that such behaviour is acceptable.

On the other hand liberal opinion in this country tends towards the view that pornography is either harmless or positively beneficial to those people who don't have sexual partners or who find it difficult to get aroused sexually. Certainly it is true that many people look at these pictures while masturbating.

It is impossible to say who is actually right about this, though it is claimed that sex crimes in Scandinavia have decreased since pornography was made legal there. One thing which is often overlooked in these discussions is the question of pornographic models. It is hard to see how young people can remain psychologically unharmed by indulging in a variety of sexual acts for the benefit of the camera. And it can't be very pleasant to consider what one's pictures are being used for.

Diseases and other problems

Venereal and sexually transmitted diseases

These are contagious diseases which are spread almost exclusively through sexual contact.

The main venereal diseases are gonorrhoea (pronounced gonoreea) and syphilis, and these, if not treated, can lead to disablement later on. During recent years there has been a gradual increase in the number of cases of venereal disease, especially of gonorrhoea, and it is thought that this increase is chiefly due to more liberal sexual attitudes among young people.

Sooner or later some of you will enter into sexual relations with people who are infected. It is always wise to watch out for the symptoms of venereal disease, as described below, and if you have the least suspicion that you have contracted anything, go to a doctor at once. That way you will avoid the disease establishing itself and infecting other people.

The doctor will either treat you personally or send you to a treatment centre. If you prefer not to consult your doctor you can go to a 'special clinic', the name given to VD clinics in hospitals. Most general hospitals have one. You will be treated with complete anonymity, and you are not obliged to name the person from whom you have caught the disease. But it is obviously wise, if you know them, to make sure they know they are infected, so that they have treatment too. And you can help prevent the spread of these diseases if you do not have intercourse again until you are definitely cured.

GONORRHOEA (clap)

Gonorrhoea is the most common form of venereal disease. In men the first symptoms are usually two to eight days after infection and take the form of an itching or smarting sensation in the urethra which becomes worse when you pass water. After the first few days a mucous secretion appears from the opening to the urethra. This discharge becomes stronger, thicker and more yellowish in colour over the following days and is a sign that the infection has spread further up into the urethra. In women the symptoms, when they are noticeable, are similar to those in men; but unfortunately for many women (and some men) there are no obvious symptoms at all. In fact, probably the best indication that a woman has the disease is that her boyfriend has it. This makes it all the more important that any symptoms should be checked at a clinic and that any person you have had sex with should be informed if infection is confirmed.

If you do not ask for treatment the symptoms may disappear of their own accord. But this does not mean that you are cured; the disease will just spread up into the sex organs unnoticed. Then, after a while, it breaks out in the form of a malignant infection of the prostate gland or the balls in men and an infection of the abdomen in women. This can result in sterility (the inability to have children) in both sexes. If you still don't get any treatment the disease may spread to the main joints (very often the knee joints) and eventually to the heart and other vital organs.

Usually gonorrhoea is *only* contracted through sexual contact, though anyone who has the disease must exercise great cleanliness and remember in particular to wash their hands after touching their sex organs, since the infection can occasionally be passed from the hands to another person's genitals.

Gonorrhoea can be cured with penicillin. It is important to return to the clinic after treatment to make certain the infection has been cured.

SYPHILIS (POX)

Syphilis is the most serious form of venereal disease and if it isn't treated can develop into a terrible disease, though as more people are diagnosed and treated early with penicillin this is gradually becoming rarer and rarer. Syphilis is almost always transmitted through sexual intercourse, though it can be passed on to lips, throat or fingers through close contact with the genitals of an infected person. It can sometimes be passed on through kissing.

Two to six weeks after infection the first stage of the disease sets in with a little sore (hard chancre), which is hard, firm and almost completely insensitive. The sore (usually only one) appears where the infection started, usually on the genitals, lips or tongue, though it may appear in other places, usually where there has been a scratch or sore. In women the chancre may be hidden inside the vagina (this applies also to men who have anal intercourse), so if you contract the disease it is important to inform anyone with whom you have had recent sexual contact, so that they will know that they need treatment as well.

Even if the disease is not treated, the sore will disappear over a couple of weeks, but this does *not* mean that you are cured. The disease then spreads steadily but unnoticed over the body. After some months it breaks out again in what is known as the second stage. This usually takes the form of a rash of red spots over the whole body and swelling in all the glands, though this swelling is most noticeable in the armpits, the groin and on the sides of the neck. At this stage some people get blisters in their mouth and a few begin to lose their hair. Even these symptoms need not seem unduly serious to the person who has the disease, though they will certainly be a worry, and again they will disappear without any kind of treatment. For the next ten to twenty years the sufferer may feel quite healthy, but eventually the disease breaks out again. This third stage is extremely serious and potentially fatal since it can affect the heart, the nervous system and the brain (leading to insanity).

NON-SPECIFIC URETHRITIS (NSU)

NSU is almost as common as gonorrhoea. It is called non-specific because it is not certain what causes it. The symptoms in men are similar to early gonorrhoea symptoms, and so is the treatment. There are rarely any symptoms in women, but they can be carriers, so it is important for any woman who has had contact with an NSU infected man to get treatment at a clinic.

In rare cases NSU can develop into a far more serious condition called Reiter's Syndrome, which is like arthritis and attacks the joints. So even if NSU is not bothering you, you should get it cured to make sure it isn't passed on.

TRICHOMONIASIS (trich)

NSU in men and trich in women often go together. Trich usually produces symptoms in women but not in men. They are: a thin yellowy-green discharge which smells nasty, particularly after inter-course, and itching and discomfort in the vagina. You should have treatment, and so should your partner, to ensure that the infection doesn't recur.

HERPES

Herpes produces little blisters in the genital area, which are usually painful, particularly when you are urinating or during intercourse. Although herpes (which is rather like cold sores in origin) can start spontaneously in some people, it is also very contagious, so it's im-portant to avoid intercourse until it has cleared up. Unfortunately there is no cure for herpes, though a doctor may be able to prescribe something to relieve your discomfort. It will eventually go of its own accord, though it may recur. Attacks often happen when you are tired or run down, so it's wise to get plenty of rest.

CRAB LICE (crabs)

Crab lice live in the hair around the genitals and are therefore gener-ally transmitted by intercourse. A crab louse can become dislodged, however, and fall on to a lavatory seat, for example, to take up residence in the next person who uses the lavatory. The lice suck blood and produce small blue marks and itching.

Crab lice will not go away no matter how thoroughly you wash and bathe. You will have to get a special solution sold by the chemist called Lorexane or Quellada. (You can get it on prescription or over the counter.) It should be left on the affected area for twenty-four hours and then washed off. It is also important to get rid of crabs on sheets, towels or clothes. They die without contact with the human body over a period of six days, so either wash all the clothes etc. with which you have had contact or simply avoid touching them for six days.

SCABIES

Scabies is caused by a tiny, almost invisible mite which lives in small burrows under the skin, particularly between the fingers, around the waist and in the armpits. The symptom of scabies is a powerful itch.

Scabies is often transmitted by sexual relations, when the bodies of two people are lying close to one another, but you can also catch it by holding hands or using other people's clothes or bed.

Scabies can be cured by applying a special solution which you can buy at a chemist. After your bath, spread the stuff all over the body (except on the head) thoroughly. You should not wash until twenty-four hours later. You must also change your sheets and underclothes. It is wise to repeat this treatment four to five days later.

VENEREAL WARTS

It is possible to contract through intercourse a virus infection which manifests itself in the form of soft, whitish, wart-like spots. These may not appear until two or three months after infection. It is important to have them removed while they are small since they can grow and become persistent.

PROTECTION AGAINST VENEREAL DISEASE

If a man uses a condom throughout intercourse it provides protection against gonorrhoea and to a certain extent against syphilis – a fact that many prostitutes discovered some time ago, which is why they will quite often demand that their clients use a condom during intercourse.

It is common practice, particularly among sailors, to rub calomel ointment on the skin on and around the sex organs immediately after intercourse in situations where there is a certain risk of catching syphilis. But, though this method is better than nothing, it does not give complete safety.

Although women can carry condoms and suggest that their partner use them, many young women would be embarrassed to do so. Spermicidal creams, pessaries or foams do provide some protection, and a cap would certainly cut down your chances of contracting gonorrhoea. Remember, though, that none of these preventive measures is fool-proof. You should still go to a clinic if your partner has a dose of VD.

And one last word for women: if you sometimes have sex with men who you don't know well and are unlikely to see again it is important to go to a clinic for periodic checks even if you have no symptoms. A disease picked up when you are young may go unnoticed at first, but it could lead to ill health and possibly sterility.

Problems affecting boys and girls

BAD BREATH

If bad breath persists without getting any better even though you brush your teeth rigorously every morning and evening, it usually means, in young people, that you either have cavities in your teeth or something wrong with your tonsils or incrustation of the nostrils. So the only thing to do is first to go to the dentist, and, if that doesn't help, to an ear, nose and throat specialist (on the recommendation of your doctor).

IMPURITIES OF THE SKIN

You may be plagued by spots and pimples for several years, and it is hardly any consolation to be told that they will disappear of their own accord as time goes by.

There are different ways of tackling the problem, but a combination of all the remedies usually gives the best results.

Your *diet* is important: fruit, vegetables, lean meat, fish, skimmed or butter milk, and low-fat cheeses will all help to clear the skin. Dairy-fat products like butter, milk, cream, chocolate and ice cream, eggs and fatty meat are all spot-makers. So it is better to avoid fried food or to use vegetable margarine or oil rather than butter or lard for frying, since vegetable products, with a few exceptions such as nuts, have less repercussions in this respect.

Fresh air, sunshine and salt water dry out spots and greasy skin. In winter a sun-ray lamp may prove a good substitute for these.

Daily attention to the skin may also be necessary. Do try to avoid picking at your spots even though you're itching to. Then, when the pimple is large and yellow you can carefully squeeze it out in a wad of cotton wool. Wash your skin with some kind of medicated soap, massaging the soap carefully right into the skin and leaving it a minute before rinsing. This should be done daily or it won't help at all. Never use propyl alcohol, ether and things like that to cleanse the skin, as these substances just remove the protective layer of fat on the skin and may even cause the spots to spread.

Blackheads are produced by the waxy wastage of the sebaceous glands. If they are allowed to remain on the skin too long they become large and dark. Before you attempt to remove the blackheads with your fingers you should wash both them and your skin with medicated soap for at least a minute; otherwise there is a danger of a spot forming in the hole left when the blackhead is removed.

HEAVY SWEATING

During puberty many young people are bothered by heavy sweating. Clean sweat does not smell nasty, but there are bacteria on the skin which can make sweat smell evil very quickly.

If you wash the parts that sweat most for at least a minute every day with a medicated soap you can prevent the sweaty smell, because the soap leaves a layer of bacteria killer on the skin.

If you sweat heavily it helps to avoid wearing synthetic fibres (nylon, acrilan, etc.) close to your skin, as these materials stop the air circulating and make the smell worse.

If thorough washing alone doesn't seem to help then you can buy an underarm deodorant at any chemist. Deodorants will not, however, replace washing. (Avoid vaginal deodorants, as they irritate the vagina.)

Problems affecting girls

MENSTRUAL DIFFICULTIES AND PAIN

Many women have trouble with their periods during the days before they are due or when they start. This may consist of: puffiness in the face, a bloated feeling in the abdomen and breasts, restlessness, irritability and a tendency to cry, or abdominal pain. Some of these problems will clear up after a few years as your periods establish themselves, but they may persist.

None of these difficulties is easily cured but they can be alleviated. Bloating and irritability are caused by excess liquid in the body. It might help to cut down on the amount of water you drink and your salt intake in the week or two before a period, and it is important to get as much sleep as possible during this time, both because you will tire more easily anyway and because you will feel more able to cope with yourself if you are rested.

The pain is caused by the muscles of your womb contracting. No one knows exactly why this happens in some women and not in others. However, again you can help yourself by: exercising (there is absolutely no need to give up sports at this time; the exercise is a positive help); some people find that herbal teas, like raspberry leaf or mint, are a help; and if you have bad pains take a couple of aspirin as soon as the pain starts, don't wait until you are doubled up in agony (regular aspirin taking is very bad for you but once a month shouldn't be a problem).

If menstrual problems are ruining your life don't just suffer: see a doctor, and insist that he or she takes you seriously. There is a lot of research being done into this at present, and in really severe cases hormone treatment might help. The contraceptive pill, incidentally, often helps period pain but it can make the other problems worse.

MENSTRUAL IRREGULARITIES

The first year you have your periods they may be irregular without there being anything abnormal. Emotional upsets, travel and pregnancy scares can also make you miss your period. If you have been having intercourse (or if any sperm has touched your vaginal area during petting) you should get a pregnancy test (p. 107) as soon as you are two weeks over-due, just to make sure. If the irregularity persists you should see a doctor.

VAGINAL DISCHARGE

From the first years of puberty onwards most girls and women have a small amount of thin, clear (or slightly cloudy) discharge from the vagina. It is quite normal, and is there to keep your vagina free of infection. A lot of discharge can be a nuisance, but it is best dealt with by washing regularly in warm water.

If the membranes in your vagina become irritated, the discharge will increase. Things like vaginal spray deodorants, strongly perfumed soaps or any form of perfume around the vaginal area may be to blame. Tights, tight trousers and nylon pants can also cause extra discharge.

If the discharge changes colour or starts to smell unpleasant you have probably got an infection and should see a doctor or go to a clinic.

One of the commonest infections of the vagina is thrush (*candida albicans*). It produces a thick white discharge and a nasty itch. The cure, which has to be prescribed by a doctor, is to insert pessaries into your vagina for about twelve consecutive nights. Sometimes thrush can recur. This could be because you didn't finish all the pessaries and the infection wasn't properly cured; or it could be that your vaginal secretions are not protecting you as they should be, in which case you should find out about preventive measures, either through a clinic or from some of the books mentioned on p. 137. Sometimes thrush occurs when you are on the pill and won't go away. In this case the best cure is a different form of contraception.

PAINS WHEN PASSING WATER

Stinging pains together with a frequent need to urinate are common symptoms of cystitis, an infection of the urethra. Some women get symptoms after the first time they have intercourse. This is due to unaccustomed pressure on the urethra and usually disappears of its own accord. However, cystitis can appear quite independently of intercourse and is often very distressing. A doctor will prescribe tablets to cure the infection but in the meantime it helps to drink as much as you can. This dilutes the urine so that it is less irritating to the urethra. Cystitis can be a recurring problem and prevention is better than cure. Clinics will usually advise on this, and some of the books mentioned on p. 137 will be useful.

If the stinging does pass away quickly it is worth keeping in mind that this is also an early symptom of gonorrhoea; if such an infection is a possibility you should go to a clinic anyway.

SORENESS IN THE WOMB

Pains in the womb can occur during or just before a period or for some women in the middle of the month, during ovulation. Period pains can be quite intense but usually have a rhythm (as though the womb was being squeezed and released). Any other pain in the womb, for example if it hurts when the penis bumps against it during intercourse, could be a sign of infection and should be investigated by a doctor. (On pain during intercourse, see also pp. 77–8.)

SCREENING FOR CERVICAL CANCER

It is important that all women who are sexually active should be screened regularly to make sure that the cells of their cervix (neck of the womb) are not changing. This test simply requires the doctor to scrape a few cells of the surface of your cervix with a spatula for examination under a microscope. It doesn't hurt, and it should be done every one to three years. If you are screened regularly any cell changes will be noted so that preventive surgery can be done to avoid the spread of malignant (cancerous) cells. Get in touch with your family planning clinic, a VD clinic (see p. 122) or your own doctor.

INVERTED NIPPLES

Some women's nipples poke inwards instead of outwards. This can present a problem with breast feeding, so pregnant women are usually shown how to massage their breasts and wear little 'shields' to make them poke out. If you find inverted nipples embarrassing you could try these methods; see books (p. 137) for more information; or you can contact the National Childbirth Trust (address on p. 136).

HAIR GROWTH

At puberty hair begins to grow gradually on the arms, legs, armpits and pubic area. Sometimes light downy hair grows also on the face and in other places. A gradual growth is usually a hereditary characteristic; but if it grows very thick or appears suddenly – possibly in conjunction with other irregularities – it may be the effect of a hormonal disorder and it would be advisable to contact a doctor.

Ordinary leg and underarm hair is often shaved off in the more northerly western countries. This is simply a cultural habit; there is certainly no medical reason for it. It is as well to remember that hair that is removed usually grows back thicker and coarser.

Other problems affecting boys

GROWTH IN THE BALLS

If one of your balls suddenly begins to grow you must go and see your doctor, even if they do not feel tender or painful. It might be due to a rupture or cyst in the scrotum (in which case it isn't actually the testicle which is growing, though it feels like it), but it might also be due to a growth in the testicle which might need to be removed by an operation.

MISSING BALLS

In small boys it is fairly common to find that one or both of the balls have not descended into the scrotum. This means that the ball will not function properly and a doctor should be consulted straight away, since it has proved necessary to operate before the child is five years old; otherwise the growth and development of the undescended testicle may be impaired.

It is also possible for one of the balls to slip up into the groin, especially if the scrotum is under pressure. In such cases you should see a doctor, who will be able to press it gently down again.

Diseases and other problems

PAIN IN THE BALLS

The balls are often very sensitive; you may even faint from the pain of a strong kick or blow directed at them.

Any disease which makes the balls swell, like gonorrhoea or mumps, will usually cause pain (but see also 'Growth in the balls' opposite).

Varicose veins in the small blood vessels around the spermatic cord may result in pain while you are running or engaged in vigorous exercise. The pains will then disappear when you are sitting still. You may find that it helps to lift up the scrotum in tight-fitting underpants or to strap it in a suspensory bandage especially made for this purpose. If it doesn't relieve the pain sufficiently then you can have a small operation to remove the varicose vein.

Some people may get pains in the balls if they are sexually excited for a long period of time without reaching a climax. An ejaculation will ease the condition, though it will disappear gradually of its own accord.

BLOOD IN THE SEMEN

Very rarely, you may find streaks of blood in the semen, after masturbation, for example. This is usually an indication that some small blood vessel has burst, which need not worry you. But it might be due to some more serious disease, so you should let the doctor examine you to make sure all is well.

FORESKIN INFECTIONS

So much smegma and urine can collect under the foreskin, particularly among men who suffer from tightness of the foreskin, that it becomes infected. The foreskin grows red and swollen; it suppurates, tickles and smarts. If you keep yourself clean under the foreskin you can avoid irritations of this kind, but obviously if the foreskin is tight it may be impossible to wash yourself properly.

Washing daily under the foreskin, if you have one, and generally keeping your genitals clean should become a habit. An infection will not only be unpleasant to you; any bacteria which you transfer into a woman's vagina can also affect her. If you do get an infection in the foreskin you will usually need medical treatment.

TIGHTNESS OF THE FORESKIN

If the foreskin fits so closely that it cannot easily be drawn back over the head of the penis, you are suffering from phimosis, or tightness of the foreskin. Almost all little boys have phimosis without there being anything abnormal about it, and by far the majority of them grow out of it. If you are well into puberty and the foreskin still isn't any looser you should go to the doctor – you must *not* try to force it back yourself. All that is needed is a small operation known as circumcision, in which part of the foreskin is removed. This is a common operation which is often performed on small boys as a preventive measure to reduce the risk of infection in later life.

SMARTING PAINS WHEN PASSING WATER

This may be one of the first symptoms of gonorrhoea (see p. 123). However, smarting pains accompanied by a frequent need to urinate can also be a sign of infection of the bladder. Both conditions require medical attention.

Useful addresses

British Pregnancy Advisory Service, First Floor, Guildhall Buildings, Navigation Street, Birmingham B2 4BT (021 643 1461): a registered charity giving advice, counselling and abortion referrals; branches all over the country.

Brook Advisory Centres, 233 Tottenham Court Road, London W1P 9AE (01 580 2991): free birth control advice and supplies, pregnancy counselling and counselling for sexual problems. Brook caters specifically for young people and has branches in many parts of the UK.

Family Planning Association, 27–35 Mortimer Street, London W1N 7RJ (01 636 7866): advice on contraception and sexual problems; mail order service for non-prescription contraceptives and books on birth control and sex education.

Family planning clinics: for free contraception advice and supplies. The address and phone number of your local clinic will be listed in your telephone directory under 'Family planning'.

Friend (01 359 7371): national advice and counselling network for homosexual men and women; you may have a service near you.

Gay Switchboard (01 837 7324): a free 24-hour service giving advice and information on a range of subjects from flat-sharing to advice centres; there may be a switchboard in your area.

Grapevine (01 607 0949): sex and contraception advice for under-thirties at 296 Holloway Road, London N7.

Irish Family Planning Association, 59 Synge Street, Dublin 8 (Dublin 682420).

Lesbian Line (01 837 8602): an advice service especially for Lesbians; ring any evening or on Monday and Friday afternoons. You can write to them at BM 1514, London WC1V 6XX.

National Childbirth Trust, 9 Queensborough Terrace, London W2 3TB (01 229 9319).

National Council for One Parent Families, 255 Kentish Town Road, London NW5 2LX (01 267 1361): helps single women before and after childbirth; also advice on adoption and single parenthood.

National Marriage Guidance Council (address in your phone book): clinics for the treatment of sexual problems. National address: Little Church Street, Rugby, Warwicks (0788 73241).

Pregnancy Advisory Service, 40 Margaret Street, London W1N 7FB (01 409 0281): provides the same sort of service as the British Pregnancy Advisory Service (see above).

Rape Crisis Centre, PO Box 42, London N6 5BU (01 340 6145): 24-hour telephone service; help, support and counselling for women who have been raped. They may be able to refer you to a centre near you.

Release, 1 Elgin Avenue, London W9 3PR (01 289 1123): a free service helping young people with a range of problems, including drugs and pregnancy.

Ulster Pregnancy Advisory Service, 338a Lisburn Road, Belfast BT9 6GH (Belfast 667345): abortion laws are stricter in Ireland; this organization sends women to England for help.

VD clinics: for your nearest clinic, look in the phone book under 'Venereal disease'.

Youth Advisory Service, 31 Nottingham Place, London W1 (01 935 1219): they can refer you to somewhere local if necessary.

Useful books

Boston Women's Health Collective, *Our Bodies Ourselves*, British edition by Angela Phillips and Jill Rakusen, Penguin, 1978. A book written by women for women, about women's sexuality and health, covering contraception, abortion, childbirth, common medical problems and more.

Brown, Paul, and Carolyn Faulder, *Treat Yourself to Sex: A Guide for Good Loving*, Dent, 1977; Penguin, 1979. A step-by-step guide to the understanding and resolution of sexual difficulties.

Brown, Rita May, *Ruby Fruit Jungle*, Corgi, 1978. A warm, funny, positive novel about lesbian relationships.

Cherniak, D., and A. Feingold, *The VD Handbook*, Montreal Health Press, 1975.

Demarest, R., and J. Sciarra, *Conception, Birth and Contraception*, McGraw Hill, 1969.

Growing Up Gay, a Youth Liberation pamphlet, 1978.

Hite, Shere, *The Hite Report*, Talmy Franklin, 1977. A survey of women's attitudes to their own sexuality.

Kaplan, Helen Singer, *The New Sex Therapy*, Penguin, 1978. Sex problems and treatment, illustrated.

Kilmartin, Angela, *Understanding Cystitis*, Heinemann, 1973. Self-help treatment for this common ailment.

McKeith, Nancy (ed.), *The New Women's Health Handbook*, Virago, 1977.

If you can't get these books locally, try Compendium, 234 Camden High Street, London NW1, or Sisterwrite, 190 Upper Street, London N1.

Index

Page numbers printed in *italic* refer to illustrations